The Day My World Caved In.

George Mwansa

First published 2009
Copyright © 2009

All rights reserved. No part of this publication may be reproduced in any form without prior permission from the publisher.

British Library Cataloguing in Publication Data. A catalogue record for this book is available from the British Library.

ISBN 1-904685-56-0

Published by The Stanborough Press, Grantham, Lincolnshire.

Printed in Thailand.
Designed by Abigail Murphy

All Scriptural quotations are taken from the New International Version.

The Day My World Caved In.

George Mwansa

Dedicated to the memory of **Cornelius Matandiko** and to **Patience Matandiko**

About the author

George Mwansa is a lecturer in the school of theology and religious studies at Solusi University, Bulawayo, Zimbabwe. He has served in the past as district pastor, Conference and Union departmental director, lecturer at the Zambia Adventist Seminary, and Communication director for the Eastern Africa and Southern Africa-Indian Ocean Divisions. As Communication director he also served as editor of *Outlook* (Eastern Africa Division general paper) and *Adventist Echo* (Southern Africa-Indian Ocean general paper). He studied at Solusi University before he went for graduate studies at Andrews University.

Acknowledgments

Since there is no such thing as writing a book single-handedly, I wish to acknowledge with thanks those who assisted in its production. May Chibende, my good friend, provided editorial help in the initial stages. My children, Mwape and Mwila, deserve mention for 'providing' a lot of scenes from which this book was written. Without their presence in my life, this book would have been like a physics or mathematics textbook. My friends, whose names you will meet, contributed also by transforming what could have been merely a historical document into a narrative. Lastly, to my heavenly Father, for life, motivation and strength to write this book, I say thank you. My Lord and Saviour, Jesus, put it well when he said: 'Apart from me you can do nothing.' (John 15:5.)

. Introduction .

In September 2005 while conducting evangelistic meetings in Chingola, Zambia, I received from someone in the audience a note that read: 'Dear Pastor Mwansa, can you please tell us how it feels to lose a wife?' In March of that same year, I had lost my wife, Martha, in a road traffic accident. The wounds of that death were still fresh and the memory vivid. I could not understand how anyone in his right mind would ask such a question. I therefore just ignored the note.

The question, 'How does it feel to lose a wife?' is not in the same category as a question regarding mathematics or physics. People respond to loss and pain differently. There is no universal formula. What I share in this book is, therefore, what I experienced when I lost my wife. While certain elements may apply in every case where loss occurs, what I share here is not exactly what everyone who loses a wife goes through. So, this is the story of what happened when I, George Mwansa, lost my wife, Martha Chibwe Mwansa.

I share this story with a view that it may help someone to hold on to God. Life without God is no life at all. Before my wife Martha died, I used to think that we were going to live a long life together. Yes, I used to think that if God allowed one or both of us to die, it would be of very old age. I also liked to entertain the idea that Jesus would come in our lifetime so we wouldn't have to die. I am sure there are many people who think like that. They see death as something that comes only to strike someone else – a neighbour, friend or colleague at work. But death is no respecter of persons. And in view of this obvious fact, we do well to have a relationship with God that guarantees us eternal life. Jesus said: 'I am the resurrection and the life. He who believes in me will live, even though he dies.' (John 11:25.)

I share this story because Martha demonstrated that it is possible to live a Christian life this side of eternity. She demonstrated through her beautiful life that victorious living is not just the domain of Bible characters, but it is something we all can enjoy.

Because I am human, you should expect to see a lot that is human in this story, a story of weakness and failure. But, thank God, Jesus Christ came into our world; therefore, the human story is also of strength – the strength that the Son of Man gives us. And victory – the victory we achieve through him who loved us and died to save us from sin.

May you be strengthened and refreshed as you read on.

The Day My World Caved In.

Contents

Chapter 1 •	6 March 2005	8
Chapter 2 •	The Bee Sting	13
Chapter 3 •	Monday 7 March	17
Chapter 4 •	Meet the Mourners	20
Chapter 5 •	Burial Day	26
Chapter 6 •	Family Meeting	35
Chapter 7 •	Details of the Accident	38
Chapter 8 •	Empty Home – 26 Hiller Rd, Gunhill	41
Chapter 9 •	'Cleansing' – *Isambwe Iyamfwa*	47
Chapter 10 •	Painful Recollections	56
Chapter 11 •	Back at the Office	59
Chapter 12 •	Advice from 'Experts'	64
Chapter 13 •	Back to the Birthplace of Our Love	66
Chapter 14 •	St Louis: meetings, music, friends, sorrow	68
Chapter 15 •	Michigan . . . Reminiscing	72
Chapter 16 •	Five Years Over; Time For Polls	80
Chapter 17 •	2005 SID Elections	87
Chapter 18 •	Back at the Office in Harare	93
Chapter 19 •	Farewell, Highlands Church Family	96
Chapter 20 •	First Anniversary of Martha's Death	100
Chapter 21 •	Remarriage; My Kids' Views	102
Chapter 22 •	The Wilderness Experience	106
Chapter 23 •	Who Was Martha Mwansa?	124

The Day My World Caved In.

chapter 1

6 March 2005.

I was driving from the Lusaka International Airport to my brother's house at 358 Independence Avenue when my mobile phone rang. Pastor Chunga of the Central Zambia Conference was at the other end. 'Pastor,' he said, 'there has been an accident in Serenje involving your family members. I have Jack, your brother-in-law, here, to speak with you.' Before I could take in the information, Jack was on the line: 'I got a phone call from Loveness in Mansa to say that Martha and Kasongo and other family members have been involved in a road traffic accident near Serenje, and that a military helicopter has been dispatched there to bring them here to Lusaka for medical attention.' My elder brother Kasongo, his wife Catherine, my wife Martha, my young brother Alex Chola and an army driver Sergeant Chisala had left that Sunday morning of 6 March for Mansa to attend the funeral of my sister Mwape, who had passed away a couple of days earlier.

My heart missed several beats as I fumbled for words of response. 'Any idea as to whether there were fatalities?' I asked. 'The information is scanty. I don't know of any other details,' Jack said. We agreed to meet at my elder brother's house along Independence Avenue, not far from the State House.

As I drove to meet Jack, my heart raced as I was wondering and worrying about many things. Questions like: 'What is Martha's condition?' 'How did the accident occur?' 'What will happen if she dies?' 'What about Kasongo and Catherine? Are they all right?' 'And Chola, has

1. 6 March 2005.

something happened to him?' No matter how hard I tried to reassure myself that God was in control of the situation, I found myself restless and worried. I arrived at my brother's house and found Jack waiting. Jack, who is Martha's elder brother, lives in Cape Town, and had come to Lusaka on business. I tried to extract as much as I could from him concerning the details of the accident, but he was equally in the dark. Strangely, he didn't look as worried as I was. He appeared calm and very composed. We learned from my brother's neighbour that the helicopter was arriving at the airport at about 6:30pm. He told us that he was going to drive there to wait for the patients. Upon their arrival he would call us so we could go to Maina Soko Military Hospital where they would be taken. My brother, a brigadier general, worked as a consultant surgeon at Maina Soko Military Hospital and he was also the director of medical services for the Zambian Army.

After an unsuccessful attempt to calm my emotions, I asked Jack if we could pray. I prayed that God would care for the accident victims and grant us peace as we waited. Despite that prayer, however, my mind was still just as restless. Surely, I thought to myself, it must have been a major accident as there was no way a helicopter could be sent to bring my folk to Lusaka. True, my brother was a senior officer in the army, but unless the victims were badly hurt a helicopter was just too expensive a means of transport. Had the time come for me to be a widower? What would happen to the kids? Surely God could not let them grow up without that important motherly love and guidance which only Martha could provide. What about my brother and his wife? Surely there was no way God would cut short their lives just like that. How would their kids cope? 'No! No! Please, God, do not let my worst fears be confirmed,' I prayed silently.

That wait – to know just what had happened – was the longest of my life. Minutes ticked agonisingly slowly. Absorbed in my silent wait, I pondered a future without Martha. The eerie silence was broken when Jack's phone rang. With hearts pounding we anxiously waited to hear who had phoned and what he was going to say. At the other end of the line my brother's neighbour, who had gone to the airport, informed us that the helicopter had landed and that we could go to Maina Soko Hospital to wait for the arrival of the ambulance. Nothing was communicated regarding the condition of the patients or whether there were any fatalities. At Maina Soko, we waited for about forty minutes

The Day My World Caved In.

before we were told to go to the University Teaching Hospital (UTH), Lusaka's main referral medical centre, where the patients were to be taken. That move heightened my anxiety. Going to the UTH meant that the victims were in a critical condition.

Upon arrival at the UTH we waited outside the entrance to the casualty wing where ambulances park. After about twenty minutes of nervous waiting we saw two ambulances approach. While their lights on top flashed, the sirens were mute. Finally both ambulances came to a standstill. The most restless moment of my life gripped my being as truth waited to confront me: Was my wife alive and if she were, what was her condition? In the front seat of the first ambulance was my elder brother. He sat as though nothing had happened to him. An impression was conveyed that he might not have been hurt badly. He had a swelling and some cuts on the face. He had a distraught and anxious look that gave the impression that something somehow was amiss. Several people, including Malita his daughter, showered him with hugs as he alighted and was helped to a wheelchair. At the back of the ambulance lay his wife on a stretcher. She was groaning with pain. A bandaged arm lay stretched with a drip hanging by the side. She was the only other occupant of that ambulance.

Seeing that my wife was not there, I quickly went to the other ambulance. At the back was my brother's driver, Sergeant Chisala. He lay quietly on a stretcher with a drip hanging by his side. He was bruised and his face appeared to be swollen. Martha and my young brother Chola were nowhere to be seen. Could they have died? I asked myself. 'I wonder where the others are,' I said to Jack. 'I am wondering the same,' Jack responded. I gathered courage and asked one of the military personnel on the scene: 'These people,' I said, 'were five in number when they left. I just wonder what could have happened to the other two?' 'I am sorry,' the man said. 'The other two died on the spot.' Words cannot adequately describe what went through my mind at that moment. Stunned, numbed and dumbfounded, knees almost giving way on me, I stood as Jack broke into an uncontrollable wail. The long wait finally culminated in what I feared most: Martha, my loving wife and friend with whom I had spent sixteen sweet years of life, was gone!

The death of my wife was too shocking to absorb. I couldn't think clearly. I just didn't know what to make of this untimely revelation. There

1. 6 March 2005.

is something about accidental death that is hard to comprehend and accept. Yes, the tragedy is abrupt and sudden. But it is the process of that death that lingers long, playing all kinds of weird images in the mind. You imagine the pain the loved one must have gone through as the vehicle rolled. You picture metal and concrete tarmac in cruel contact as trapped, innocent people are hit and knocked from every side. You imagine the desperate cry for help as the victim struggles to hold on to life. Lacerations, swellings, broken or – even worse still – amputated limbs, turning an attractive person into a zombie. True, we must all at some point go the way of all the living, but why go this way? Why not a better and more dignified way? The once beautiful body of my wife, I thought, now lying without dignity in a mortuary 400km from where I stood. True, the dead know nothing, yet the corpse of a loved one is indeed still a loved one. Bleak winter settled over my soul.

Bad news in most cases travels faster than good news. My niece Betty Mumba, public relations officer for the Drug Enforcement Commission, had received the news of the accident and was among the first to arrive at the hospital. She came where I stood and hugged me as she burst into tears. Next came Mr and Mrs Rushford Musonda of the Adventist Church headquarters in Lusaka. I told them about the death of my wife and both were too stunned and numbed to utter words. We hugged as tears freely flowed. In the confusion of that moment it is difficult to remember other people who came.

We had to move to the next location, the Adventist Church offices, to make phone calls and contact people who needed to know what had happened. The Musondas offered me a lift. Pastor Cornelius Matandiko, the president of the Adventist Church in Zambia, and Pastor Harrington Akombwa, executive secretary, joined us at the office. We contacted Pastor Pardon Mwansa and Mr Jannie Bekker, president and treasurer respectively of the Adventist Church in the Southern Africa-Indian Ocean Division. They being my leaders had to be notified immediately. Mwansa, shocked to hear the news, spoke with me briefly and promised to call later. He and Bekker were in Gaborone, Botswana, attending meetings.

Later, the three officers, Matandiko, Akombwa and Musonda, left me briefly to discuss some matters by themselves. Emerging from that meeting they told me that the funeral was going to be held at the Matandikos' home. They felt that it was inappropriate to host the funeral

The Day My World Caved In.

at my brother's house as he and his wife were both in hospital. When we left the office, I was led to Mr Musonda's house inside the compound of the Adventist Church headquarters. Outside, we found a group mostly of women who had gathered waiting to see me and share their grief. Each hugged me as she wept. Inside the Musondas' house I sat as people kept coming in to give their condolences. I sat there in a dazed silence, well aware that the night was going to be long.

Finally, Mr Musonda announced that it was time to move to Pastor and Mrs Matandiko's house, located about 5km from where we were, in a neighbourhood known as Presidential Housing Initiative (PHI). We arrived and found the house ready for us. As usual, on such occasions, the sofas, coffee table, stereo rack and other big items in the living room had all been removed to create space for mourners. We found the room half full. When I entered, women broke into wailing. I sat and bowed my head as I contemplated the fate that awaited me in the future. I had started that day as a married man. Then, unexpectedly, I had become a widower! For a time, I reasoned, I was going to be the centre of negative attention. Everywhere I went people would stare at me and whisper, 'Behold the man who has lost a wife.' An indescribable emotional pain gripped me, causing me to wonder whether there was any meaning to life.

2. The **Bee Sting** .

• chapter 2

The
Bee Sting .

I marvelled to myself, how life could change so quickly. The events of the past few days passed before me as in a panoramic view. It was Thursday 3 March when Pastor Pardon Mwansa, his mother, his maid and I left Harare at about 2pm for Lusaka, Zambia. Earlier that morning I was scheduled to fly to Lusaka but found all the flights fully booked. My good friend Pardon was going to be driving his mother back to Lusaka that afternoon. I had resisted the temptation to travel with him, because only a few days earlier I had driven from Pretoria, South Africa, with Martha and some friends. And a week before that I had driven to and from Chingola, Zambia. Clearly the driving option was simply out. But there was only one flight to Lusaka that day and it was fully booked. I decided, therefore, to get a lift with my good friend Pardon.

Mwansa and I sat in front while his mother and the maid sat at the back. Apart from the occasional problem with the cooling system of the vehicle, the trip was without incident. But somewhere along the way a bee from nowhere just flew inside the car, stung me on the arm and dropped to the floor. In retaliation I crushed it with my foot. I told the others in a matter-of-fact tone about the incident. As far as I could remember, this was the first time I had been stung by a bee. Mwansa's mother at the back made a casual comment: 'A bee sting, my son, is a sign of good luck.' We all laughed about it and wondered how something as painful as a bee sting could be a sign of good luck. We drove on and forgot about the incident, and engaged our thoughts on more important

The Day My World Caved In.

issues. There was nothing about that trip worth mentioning, apart from the fact that God guided us safely to Lusaka.

We arrived in Lusaka after 7:30pm and went to visit Pardon's young sister, Fordina, where his mother was to stay for a couple of days before proceeding to Mansa, her final destination. Fordina and her husband not only welcomed us but treated us to a sumptuous dinner. Later, Pardon received a phone call from his wife Judy in Harare. Because of the noise, he went to take that phone call outside. Minutes later, he came back to announce to the group that Mwape, my sister, who had been quite ill, had passed away. There was silence as each of us digested the sad news. Pardon, who had a pressing church appointment in Gaborone, Botswana, left the following day.

Mwape was child number five and the older of the two sisters in my family. She was born long after my mum had most likely given up on having a daughter. Dad used to tell how frustrated and disappointed Mum used to feel about the fact that we didn't have a female child in the family. 'Your family is headed for extinction,' she would say. Among Bemba-speaking people who are matrilineal, the female child is very important. Through her the family grows. It was thus natural that when Mwape was born in 1970 my Mum was very happy. Mwape's other name 'Kumbwako' (Admire), which she did not like, demonstrated Mum's joy at the turn of events. Mwape, unfortunately, had three failed marriages and the only child she ever had died in infancy.

A week before Mwape's death, I had received a phone call from my cousin Paul in Mansa that Mwape's condition had deteriorated. 'It's just a matter of days,' Paul had said. In December 2004 I travelled to Mansa to see Mwape. At that time she had shown remarkable signs of recovery. Apart from praying together, we reflected on a number of life's issues. She appreciated that visit as well as the one my wife made when she went to see her a few weeks prior to that. Mwape had finally answered the call that awaits each of us. Because we all knew that unless the Lord intervened she would go, the announcement of her death was not as shocking as that of my wife.

That same evening I phoned my wife to discuss details of the funeral arrangements. We agreed that she would drive the following day (Friday 4 March) from Harare with my brother Alex Chola. We would then travel to Mansa together, hopefully, the following day. Driving to Mansa, a

2. The Bee Sting.

distance of about 1,300km from Harare, was going to be costly. I entertained the possibility of just sending my dad some money to help with funeral costs.

On the morning of Friday 4 March, I phoned my cousin Paul in Mansa to inquire about plans for burial and also to test whether the idea of just sending money would be appropriate. I asked Paul to consult my dad about that possibility. Dad felt that the idea was OK. He told me that since my other brother Kasongo and his wife were travelling, they would represent us. Just to make sure I was not committing a cultural blunder, I went to see Mr Musonda, treasurer for the Adventist Church in Zambia and a man well versed in Bemba traditions and culture. Mr Musonda agreed that sending money to help with funeral expenses was a good idea. 'It's not possible and practical that every funeral that occurs a working man like you must always attend.' In the afternoon of that same day my wife and my brother Chola arrived from Harare. I informed my wife of the new arrangements. However, I also mentioned that my elder brother and his wife were going to drive to Mansa. 'In that case,' my wife responded, 'since I am already here, I would like to travel with them if there will be space.'

So it was that on Sunday 6 March, very early in the morning, my brother Brigadier General Kasongo Mwansa, his wife Catherine, his driver Sergeant Chisala, my wife Martha, and my young brother Alex Chola started off for Mansa. The army jeep Cherokee they initially used gave them problems on the way. When they reached Kabwe (about 176km from Lusaka), they left the Cherokee and hired another vehicle at Kohima Barracks. Four hundred kilometers from Lusaka near Serenje the accident occurred in which my young brother and my wife perished.

I sat there in the funeral house wondering why I had not persuaded my wife not to travel to Mansa in view of the fact that my dad had agreed for us just to send some money to help with the funeral expenses. I also reflected on the fact that perhaps the tragedy would have been avoided if we had just driven our car to Mansa. True, it was going to be expensive, yet not as expensive as losing a brother and a wife. In the meantime, scores of people kept trooping in. Those who were in doubt as to whether it was true that Martha – Pastor George Mwansa's wife – had passed away saw me seated with my head bowed low. The mood in the house was too sombre to allow for talking. Occasionally a woman here

The Day My World Caved In.

and there overcome with shock and grief would burst into uncontrollable weeping. I heard a woman cry: 'Martha, how can you do this to your husband and the children? And the singing ministry with your husband, what will become of it? Oh, Martha, how can you do this to us?' Those piercing words broke my heart. I thought, how true the lamentation! Martha was the human pillar in our family. With her ill-timed departure to the land of the dead, life undoubtedly was going to make a difficult turn for us.

My mind turned to Justin Chapuswike, my cousin, who is also a pastor in the Adventist Church. About two years earlier, he had also lost his wife through an illness. Then I knew in part what the young pastor must have been feeling the day he sat surrounded by mourners as I was seated now. Far away in Cape Town at Helderberg College he had gone to pursue his theological studies. I wasn't sure he had heard the news of the death of my wife. However, bad news being always swift to fly, chances were he might have heard by then.

Some time later that night, Pastor Matandiko called me to one of the bedrooms and told me to rest there. I sat on the bed with a couple of people by my side. By that time news of Martha's death had travelled far and wide. Friends and acquaintances were phoning from everywhere, using either Pastor Matandiko's or Mr Musonda's numbers. By midnight I switched off the light and put my emotionally exhausted body on the bed. I lay there, lost in my chaotic world, wondering what good could come out of that experience.

chapter 3

Monday 7 March.

Monday 7 March, I awoke to the fact that I was a widower. 'You have no wife, buddy,' the inner voice whispered. I wondered what I should do. As I had no strength even to pray, I hoped others would be guided by God to do so on my behalf. I wanted to go and take a shower before most people were up, but I wondered whether that would be appropriate. I once heard that in my culture *mukamfwilwa* (widow or widower) is not allowed to do certain things during a funeral. Not being well versed in such traditions myself, and having no one by my side to guide me, I was not sure whether taking a shower was one of those prohibited things. Though I was careful not to offend people, I saw nothing wrong in taking a shower. I thus proceeded to take one. The issue of wearing perfume confronted me next. I knew that some people might get offended by something as trivial as wearing perfume. 'How does a grieving person apply perfume?' they would argue. However, knowing that many people would be coming to hug me that day as a way to express their condolences, I chose to apply the roll-on deodorant and wear a light perfume. Body odour is offensive; let's face the facts.

Up to that point, I had no idea about the condition of my brother, his wife and the driver at the hospital. Early that day some of our church leaders visited them and brought an encouraging report of my brother and his wife. The driver, they said, was still not able to speak. They had all been taken to the Intensive Care Unit of the University Teaching Hospital.

After protracted negotiations with members of my family and those of

The Day My World Caved In.

my wife, it was agreed that the burial should take place in Lusaka. Negotiations for the place of burial almost turned ugly when key relatives from both families living quite far from Lusaka cited travel expenses as constraints they could not easily overcome. We compromised by agreeing to foot the travel expenses of key people we felt should attend. We were very grateful that they were willing to accommodate our view. That would make it easier for those who wished to travel from Zimbabwe, Botswana, Malawi and South Africa to come to the funeral. Lusaka being the capital city would prove more central for those who wished to attend the funeral from any part of the country.

Mwape, my sister who had passed away earlier that week, prompting the trip that caused the accident in which my wife and brother died, was being buried that day. It was hoped that some relatives of mine living in Mansa and those of my wife living in Nkumbi (home of my mother-in-law about 900km from Lusaka) would travel to Lusaka on the Tuesday. Life, they say, is stranger than fiction. Who would have imagined the death of my sister Mwape would bring in its train such a tragedy? I was reminded of a real life story I was told by Besa, a niece of my late wife. It was about Esther, a friend of hers, whose family shared a similar tragedy. A relative had died far from where Esther's family lived. Esther, her mum, dad, sister, brother-in-law and grandmother were travelling on a mini-bus to Choma to attend the funeral of their relation. Somewhere near Kapiri-Mposhi, a tyre burst, causing the vehicle to roll, killing on the spot Esther's parents, grandmother and brother-in-law.

I pondered how the news of the death of Martha and Chola was taken at the funeral of Mwape. A funeral within a funeral, I thought. The focus had suddenly to shift from one who had died from an illness to those who had died suddenly and unexpectedly in an accident.

In the afternoon of that day, Pastor Pardon Mwansa and Mr Jannie Bekker arrived from Botswana. Pastor Mwansa was not only a colleague but had been a friend of mine since childhood. More than that, he had known Martha from childhood, as his and Martha's family were friends. Mwansa, therefore, came not only as head of the Southern Africa-Indian Ocean Division where both Martha and I worked, but also as a friend. Mr Bekker, treasurer of the same institution, was someone I had come to know in 2002. Before he came to work as head of the treasury department, he was treasurer of the Adventist Church in South Africa,

3. Monday 7 March.

Lesotho, Swaziland and Namibia. Bekker is a man whom you soon get to like. He is a kind, thoughtful and generous man. His sense of humour makes his administration pleasant to deal with. I had no doubt that Bekker's coming was more from a sense of friendship than from duty as an administrator.

Bekker hugged me as he came into the room where I was. He offered his condolences and sat down. Mwansa was too stunned and shocked, I guess, to offer any embrace. He simply stood there, shook my hand and proceeded to sit down. Silence is often golden in moments like these. After Mwansa and Matandiko had left to consult on certain matters, Bekker, alone with me, spoke about the deep loss he felt at the death of Martha. He spoke about the wonderful person he had found Martha to be, not just as a worker at the office but as a pastor's wife. He encouraged me to be strong and close to the kids.

In the evening, many who had come to learn of the tragedy arrived. Inside and outside, the house was teeming with mourners. It was practically impossible for me to go outside. I had to be in a room by myself to receive mourners. They walked in – male and female, young and old – to offer their condolences. Many came in weeping while others just sat and cried. I received phone calls from friends in many parts of the world. Some openly wept as they struggled to find words to comfort me. In the living-room many gathered and sang. The majority of mourners sat outside where discussions ranged from Martha's death to politics and any other subject of interest. Though I was slowly beginning to digest the fact that Martha was gone and I would not be able to see her this side of eternity, the pain of loss was nevertheless just as intense as it had been on Sunday when I received the news. I cannot remember at what point I drifted into dreamland. I know, though, that it took a while for me to find sleep.

The Day My World Caved In .

• chapter 4

Meet the Mourners .

By Tuesday 8 March, almost the entire world that knew me and Martha had learned about her death. Technology's cyber world and its sister telephone network had displayed their brilliant communication feat by compressing the world into a global village. Asia, Europe, America, Africa and Australia, all became aware of the death of Martha. Friends, relatives, acquaintances and church workers from around the world were all shaken with the news of Martha's sudden death. Very early in the morning, the two bodies were brought from Serenje and taken to Ideal Funeral Home Parlour to await burial the following day, Wednesday.

That day we anticipated the arrival of many of those travelling from distant places: relatives and friends from Luapula (one of Zambia's provinces where both my people and those of Martha lived), the Copperbelt (another of Zambia's provinces), Zimbabwe, Botswana, South Africa, Malawi and other areas. I cannot remember the order in which those people arrived: suffice it to say when each lot came there was fresh mourning.

In the contingent that came from the Copperbelt, I think of Besa, Martha's niece. Weeping uncontrollably, her eyes popping out and her body shaking, she asked loudly: 'What have we done to deserve this?' Joyce, her auntie, sat close to me, crying with all the intensity she could muster. They were clearly at a loss to make sense of this tragedy. And they were not the only ones. It was as if the whole world were reeling in shock. Mr Ezekiel Musangu, a distant relative of Martha, wept as though

4. Meet the Mourners.

the end of the world had come, finding him on the wrong side. Christine, Martha's young sister, was in a state hard to describe. Her voice had almost gone after what appeared to be unstoppable crying. Her legs being unable to support her frame, she was made to sit down. She walked us through her lamentation, leaving no one to doubt how sad and grieved she was at the sudden death of her sister.

Martha and Christine grew up together like twins. In June 1985, after graduating from Solusi University, I was sent to the small mining town of Kalulushi to work as a district pastor. I found Martha and Christine living with their sister Loveness. Whenever I visited their home as a pastor (and believe me, at that point I had no other motives) they provided great company. Though I could not enter into the heart of Christine to see what issues she was grappling with, I could tell that she was terribly affected by the loss of the one she loved so much.

Pastor Kapambwe from Chingola wept like a small girl who had lost her most treasured possession. Mr Bodwin Chishimba from Kitwe stood and looked at me before he broke into a wail that drowned out all the other mourners. Others, men and women, just joined in and let out their pent-up emotions. Though I had gone through several sobbing episodes of my own, I could not hold my tears in this free-for-all emotional outburst.

The group that came from Luapula, comprising my relatives and those of Martha, increased, if possible, our sense of loss. My dad was the first to walk into the room where I was. Crying like a man mourning for his wife, he sat on the floor and put the blame for the death of Martha on Mwape, the daughter he had buried the previous day. 'Why did you not just go alone?' he asked through tears. 'Why did you have to take the lives of innocent people?' Then he reminded himself about the death of his wife (my mother) who had left him almost three years earlier. 'Oh, my dear wife, why did you leave me to suffer like this?' He surely could not help but wallow in self-pity. The man had lost a daughter, son and daughter-in-law in a space of less than a week.

My mother-in-law came in and hugged me through sobs. With her head bowed low, she wept silently, too tired and overcome with grief to utter words. The news of Martha's tragic accident had dropped like a bomb, sudden and destructive. I sensed that she was still in denial and too shocked, perhaps, to believe Martha was gone. The tragedy was just

The Day My World Caved In.

something beyond anyone's capacity to comprehend and handle.

When the people from the office in Harare arrived, the truth of Martha's death slowly began to sink in, as they found mourners crowded everywhere, inside and outside the house. Alice, Shingirai, Maria, Patience, Good-son, Abisha, Ruthy, Jacinta, Solomon, Judith, Effie, Denise, all came and hugged me through sobs. Judith, Pardon's wife, embraced me tightly as she wept for a friend she was no longer going to talk to in this world. We all sat there expressing our emotions the best we knew how. My eleven-year-old son Brainerd Mwila, also in that group, came and hugged me and sat for a while before he went out. I could only think of how unfortunate he was to have to grow from that point without that important motherly touch and guidance. I counted myself blessed that God had spared me the grief of losing a mother at an early age.

My good friends from Malawi, Mwewa Chibende, his wife May and Gertrude Mfune, arrived in the afternoon. It had taken them one-and-a-half days to cover the stretch from Blantyre to Lusaka. Though this is a long stretch, they could have taken a day had they started off early in the morning. May clung to me through sobs. To say that May had been close to Martha is an understatement. May was the first woman Martha learned to be close to when we got married. Our two families then lived at Rusangu Mission in Monze. I was a Bible teacher at Rusangu Ministerial School while Mwewa, May's husband, was the treasurer for the South Zambian Field of Seventh-day Adventists.

Our two young families were so tightly knit that life could not have been better. We had Bible studies three times every week and often ate our meals together. I have never forgotten the impact of those Bible studies upon our lives. Our salaries were low, very low indeed, and we had very little in terms of material possessions, yet we had the most wonderful time of our lives. Today we often look back to that period and wonder how we could have been so happy with so little. From that cradle, Martha and May developed, nursed and nurtured a relationship that one rarely finds these days. Just two weeks prior to this tragedy, our two families were reunited in Pretoria where we had gone to attend a camp meeting for professionals and business people. You should have been there to see how the two 'girls' consumed that time with what we men term as women's small talk. You should have been there to see how they relished choosing meticulously the appropriate attire for each of the

4. Meet the Mourners.

days we were there. They chose the front seats in the large St George's Hotel Convention Centre. To say that they looked pretty is not only being economical with words but to reveal a lack of knowledge of the English language.

That world — Martha's and May's — created beautifully, and seemingly indestructible, had, in the twinkling of an eye, been crushed and was about to be dumped into the dustbin of history. From hence May would always say, at least until Jesus returns to this Earth, that 'I used to have a wonderful friend by the name of Martha Mwansa.'

Yes, May held me tightly as she mourned the death of her friend. As her pent-up emotions found their release through tears, my mind was taken back to that time when May came into our lives. It was like watching a DVD of our life with the Chibendes from its inception to this point. I could not comprehend how such a moving and thrilling real-life movie could come to such a tragic conclusion. Why would the director of this movie, God in this case, choose to conclude it this way? It was a puzzle, riddled with all kinds of unanswered questions. May continued to cry. Suddenly a flood of emotions swept over me. Covering my face with my hands, I started crying. Mwewa, May's husband, whose eyes were also red by then, put his hand around my shoulders as May held me even tighter. We cried and just cried like little kids, not caring who was watching.

At about 2:30pm, Pardon, Cornelius, his wife Patience and several friends of ours escorted me to the airport to pick up Mwape, my fifteen-year-old daughter studying at Maxwell Adventist Academy in Nairobi. I shuddered to contemplate the reaction of Mwape upon hearing that her mother had died. Earlier, word had been sent to her school authorities about the tragic accident. They were asked to tell Mwape only that her mother had been involved in a car accident in Zambia and that she, therefore, needed to travel there. It was felt that the news of her mother's death would be too traumatising to reveal before she arrived in Zambia, especially as she was going to be travelling alone.

Mwape has always been a quiet girl from the time she was born. Often if she has nothing to do she will go to her bedroom to listen to music or some other such teenage preoccupation. She has the unique habit of talking only when it is necessary. If you don't know her well, you will be fooled into thinking she doesn't talk. I have also come to realise that this

The Day My World Caved In.

quiet girl takes after me. Those who don't know me well often complain about 'this proud, quiet and unfriendly guy.' A lady from Uganda, who had known me only through casual contacts in committee meetings, one day came and told me that she had a confession to make. I was in Kampala with several workmates from Harare conducting meetings for our church workers. After hearing the presentations I made and coming to know me slightly better, she had this to say: 'You know, Pastor Mwansa, I have always held you to be a proud and quiet person who doesn't like talking to people. But after interacting with you these few days, I want to confess that I had a wrong picture of who you are.' I laughed and told her that she was not the only one who supposed me to be that way. 'Many others who don't know me well have said the same thing,' I said. 'Those who know me well will always argue that George isn't a quiet person.' I guess what I am saying is that perhaps Mwape is the same.

When Mwape finally arrived, she was wearing a smile revealing dimples on her beautiful cheeks. How sad, I thought, knowing that in a matter of minutes her world would crumble into pieces which none of us present would be able to remake. After the hugs were over, Pardon and I called her aside to break the news which we were all reluctant and dreading to share: 'Your mother,' I said, almost breaking into tears, 'died in a road accident on Sunday.' She looked at me in disbelief and asked: 'Is she dead, really dead?' I said, 'Yes.' Her eyes popped wide open as her face, which a few minutes before had been bright with a smile, crumpled with pain. Her legs were wobbling. I quickly held her as she burst into tears. I tried desperately to hold my own tears in check but I could not. People had told me repeatedly to be strong 'for the sake of the kids', but that advice just disappeared like mist from the air. Suddenly, I was overcome with emotions too deep to express. My daughter had lost a mother and friend whom she related to so well. And being a man, I could not fill the void my wife's death had created, no matter how hard I tried. Some things can be understood only by women, in the same manner that other things can be understood only by men.

As we drove back to Pastor Matandiko's house where the funeral was being held, I tried hard to control my emotions, but tears just kept flowing freely. Mwape sat between Pardon and me while Cornelius drove with his wife Patience sitting in the front passenger's seat. Empty and

4. Meet the Mourners.

hopeless thoughts kept criss-crossing the dry landscape of my mind, leaving only a trail of desperation and helplessness. To make matters worse, I could not figure out what was going on in Mwape's mind as she sat there trying to come to terms with the news she had just received. Death which, hitherto, had been the portion of only a selected unlucky few had knocked at her door, showing that no one was untouchable. 'Now that I have taken your mother,' Death seemed to have been saying to Mwape, 'you can be sure that I am coming after your father. You'd better watch out, kid, for nothing can stand in my way.' Silence reigned throughout the drive to the funeral house.

Naturally, some people started crying as soon as we arrived. I can only imagine what they might have been thinking: 'Poor father and daughter, what becomes of them now? How will they cope?' We went straight inside the house as scores of people turned their eyes to see how we were coping. Patience Matandiko took Mwape to her bedroom and had her sit there as I retired to my room. Meanwhile, people kept pouring in to offer their condolences.

In the evening, more people kept coming, making Matandiko's medium-sized yard look shrunken. A number of singing groups from around Lusaka came to show their solidarity. A preaching service was also organised.

Because of the many people who kept phoning, wanting to talk with me, I gave my cousin Justin, who had arrived earlier that day on a flight from Johannesburg, the phone so he could respond to many of the calls. Justin basically determined which I could take and which he would answer. A number of callers were not in a position to hold back their emotions. I listened as they cried over the phone, wondering myself what response I was to give. While many of the people could not find the words to speak, I found myself in an equally awkward position, not knowing what to say. An announcement was made that the burial would take place at Libala Adventist church the following day, Wednesday, at 9am. As a result of seeing so many people and sitting too long in the room, I felt so tired that when the time to sleep came I felt very relieved.

The Day My World Caved In.

chapter 5

Burial Day.

Wednesday morning, 8 March, I took an early bath and wore a black suit and white shirt in preparation for the burial. During the previous evening, we had agreed that a few people from both families would join me and the kids to have a private body viewing at the Ideal Home Funeral Parlour. We decided to do that to allow for an unhurried viewing of the bodies.

We waited inside the funeral parlour for about thirty minutes before we were finally ushered to the room where the bodies lay. Martha, the wonderful woman I had spent sixteen blessed years with, lay there in a sleep she would not wake from until Jesus' coming. Her head appeared puffed up while one of her eyelids looked slightly swollen. Despite the slight contortions on her face, she wore a serene look. Never more would I have the privilege to speak to her until the trumpet of the Lord would sound. Then my beautiful angel would wake up, not in the distorted manner in which the devil had decided she would go but in a transformed body, no longer capable of succumbing to death.

Then I turned to the other coffin where my brother Alex Chola lay. He appeared bruised and cut all over. His swollen face must have received the bluntest of the knocks and cuts. I imagined the agony the young man must have gone through as the vehicle tumbled and rolled. Later, I was told by Jack, who had identified him at the mortuary in Serenje, that his neck had almost been severed. His head simply clung to the body by some thin thread of muscle. The devil is a cruel monster.

5. Burial Day .

My elder brother General Kasongo and I had helped Chola to do a course in video production in Lusaka. A few months earlier, he had graduated from that course with distinction. I had invited him to stay with us as we tried to chart the way forward. At that time, he had helped to film a television programme, *The Bible Speaks*, that we had just started. He also served as the main cameraman for a new video album I was working on. He showed such passion and commitment to his new-found career that I was convinced the sky was going to be his only limit. I wondered how a man just starting to live his life could end it so tragically. What, I asked, was God's purpose in creating him? What lessons had he left for us? I could only hope the few months we had lived with him had meant much in his walk with God. At home he had learnt to interact with Besa, Chisha, Mwila, John, Martha and me. We had all been one great family who enjoyed living together.

Tears flowed freely from many who were in the room that morning. Strangely, I stood there strong enough to live through the whole ordeal without shedding any tears. I had earlier mentioned to Pardon that I wanted to say something after everyone had viewed the bodies. But it became clear that that wasn't going to be possible, in view of the fact that some were openly weeping and could not bear the agony of the moment. However, once we had all come out and were seated in the small chapel of the funeral parlour, I asked Pardon if I could be allowed to say a few words. Those who were in the room included my dad, my kids, Judy, my mother-in-law, Justin, Mr Jannie Bekker and other close relatives. I proceeded to take my position and paused for some seconds, composing myself before I began to speak.

'This is a sad day for all of us,' I said, my voice breaking. 'The woman with a distorted face who sleeps in the casket has been a wonderful person.' I paused as a sea of emotions engulfed me, making me break into tears. In those few seconds I stood there it was as though her whole life – her wonderful life – passed before me. I thought, 'I will never ever bask in the sunshine of this wonderful woman's life.' What a terrible loss this would be! Martha had been an incredibly wonderful wife, friend and mother. I struggled to get myself back on track but it was of no use. The flood of emotions was too strong to arrest at that point. Pardon quickly came and helped me as we both staggered out to a waiting car.

Two casket-carrying vehicles with flashing lights led our convoy to

The Day My World Caved In.

Libala church where mourners had gathered for a service. I had never once even imagined that life would bring an occurrence of that tragic magnitude in my path. Tears continued to flow, making the tissue I was using to wipe them away almost unusable. I prayed silently that God would dry away the tears before we reached the church. For almost the whole ten minutes it took us to arrive, my red eyes continued to bathe in tears. Then the tears stopped about a kilometre before I entered the church, though it was obvious that I had been crying.

Libala Adventist church is big. The place was packed, leaving hardly any space for seating. The intense heat did not help matters. We took our places as we waited for the bodies to be brought in. Women clad in uniform marched in from the back, singing and bearing the two coffins.

Pastor Cornelius Matandiko, leader of the Adventist Church in Zambia, stood to preach what must undoubtedly have been a difficult message. Cornelius is not just a colleague in the ministry; he is also a very wonderful friend of mine. I first met Cornelius at Solusi University when we both studied theology there. He has a cool and calm personality which makes him a darling to many. His sense of humour is unmatched. I doubt whether the guy has any enemies. Pastor Solomon Maphosa, leader of the Adventist Church in Zimbabwe, who was a classmate of ours, has always maintained that Cornelius and I were the noisiest guys on the campus of Solusi. I doubt whether he is far from telling the truth. Cornelius and I were very noisy people, often to the point of even annoying others. We would shout across campus looking for each other: 'Tata, tata,' (literally meaning, father, father). In the library, while others were studying, we would often break the silence by calling each other 'tata'. Some people even questioned whether we were studying for the ministry. Undoubtedly, some students questioned whether we were going to last long in the ministry. One afternoon after making a lot of noise on campus, Cornelius justified it by observing: 'You know, tata, this is the only time we can make noise by ourselves. When we go back home to work as pastors, it will not be possible to do so.'

That shouting game of ours might actually have been carried too far. One time when school closed, I travelled to Lusaka, Zambia, and left Cornelius on campus. He was going to follow several days later. We agreed that I would wait for him at the Lusaka Railway Station from where we would proceed to the Copperbelt (a province in Zambia where

5. Burial Day .

copper is mined). I asked how I was going to know in which coach he was riding. He told me that he would simply shout 'tata,' 'tata,' from his coach. We agreed that that would be the best way to locate each other. It would, after all, provide some fun, with people seeing a big man like him shouting the tata slogan. Well, when the day in question came, Cornelius did indeed arrive. And he went ahead shouting like a mad person at the Lusaka Railway Station. 'Tata,' 'tata,' 'tata,' 'tata!' Unfortunately, I was nowhere to be seen. Cornelius told me later that he was very disappointed that I had failed to keep my promise. Every time he wants to stress the point that I don't keep promises, he refers to that incident.

Later, after we had both served in the ministry for more than five years in Zambia, we went to the Seventh-day Adventist Theological Seminary at Andrews University, Berrien Springs, Michigan, for further studies. I could talk about life there; sufficient to say we had a wonderful time together.

Cornelius is a fine preacher. In his sermons he has this gift of weaving humour that makes him hammer his points home effectively and pointedly. On that solemn day he spoke about Christ's words to his disciples in John 14:1-3. 'Do not let your hearts be troubled. Trust in God; trust also in me. In my Father's house are many rooms; if it were not so, I would have told you. I am going there to prepare a place for you. And if I go and prepare a place for you, I will come back and take you to be with me that you may be where I am.' Cornelius made the point that the Earth had no room for the departed ones. 'The earth no longer needs them,' he argued; 'that's why they are no more. But Jesus says that in his Father's house are many rooms. Our departed friends have simply slept to await the moment Jesus will usher them into the many rooms he has gone to prepare.' He continued: 'I just imagine how it will be meeting Martha in the air. I am sure Martha will ask me jokingly: "So what did you talk about at my funeral?" ' Numbed with grief, confused and exhausted with reflective listening, I sat on the hard wooden pew as Cornelius preached to a packed congregation.

After the sermon, the two caskets were opened to allow mourners to view the bodies. As usual during such times, there are those who can't stomach the pain and simply break into uncontrollable weeping while others collapse from shock. Fordina, Pardon's young sister, could not face the ordeal. Throwing herself on the ground, she broke down and wept uncontrollably. She lay prostrate, body shaking, giving rise to fears that

The Day My World Caved In.

she was going to pass out.

As mourners filed to view the bodies, I saw a good number of people from my church at Highlands in Harare and elsewhere. My pastor Jonathan and his wife Judy Musvosvi were also there. Pastor Solomon Maphosa, president of the Adventist Church in Zimbabwe, and Pastor Evans Muvuti, executive secretary, had driven from Bulawayo to show support. Pastor Ben Strike, president of the Adventist Church in the South Botswana Conference, and his wife Priscilla were there. Mr Dibden Chileya, executive secretary of the Adventist Church in the North Botswana Field, and his wife Prisca also attended. My secretary Elize Hibbert and her husband Julian were there, and a number of people from Highlands Adventist church in Harare.

After a long time when all the people had passed through, the close family members were allowed to view the bodies once more. I took one long last look into the face of the woman who had been my joy for sixteen years. 'Blessed are those who die in the Lord,' the Bible says. 'May their works follow them.' Martha had fought the good fight and finished the race. She had kept the faith. Henceforth a crown of life which the Lord, the righteous Judge, has promised would be hers the moment she would wake up. We had one more look and finally the casket was closed. It was time to go to the cemetery at Leopards Hill.

Our car was third in a long convoy of vehicles. Ahead of the ones in front carrying the coffins was a police traffic controller on a motorbike. As he swept the cars ahead to give us adequate space to manoeuvre, I contemplated the meaning of life on Earth. Martha was going to turn forty in May 2005 and they say life begins at forty. And if life starts at that age, how could it end without her even reaching that age? If that statement is not true – and it is not – what about the one from the Word of God that says that man's allotted years are seventy? What would one make of that statement? Martha's skin was fresh and her beauty so evident that she was often mistaken for a twenty-something or early-thirty-something girl. What purpose, really, did it serve to take away such a young and very promising life? Leaving aside beauty which, they say, is only skin deep, this was a woman deeply committed to serving God and man. I say this as one who knew her intimately. My friend Pardon in trying to understand why such an 'unnecessary' death had to occur could only say: 'Such a wonderful person didn't deserve to die.'

5. Burial Day.

I had seen people driving in columns similar to ours many times, but did not think my turn would come so early and abruptly. I knew, of course, that some day our turn would come, but I didn't think it would come so suddenly and so tragically. Life being what it is, at the time we were escorting our loved ones to the grave, mourning the deep loss that had occurred, others were rejoicing in receiving loved ones who had just been born. That day, perhaps, some were even discussing wedding plans. A day of gloom and sadness for us was to them a day of great rejoicing.

Finally we arrived at the place of rest for our two departed ones. Fresh graves stood there waiting to receive death's latest victims. Earth, what an angry and hungry consumer you are! Pastor Dimas Chende, the man who baptised me, used to have a sermon on the Earth being one of those 'things that don't get satisfied no matter how many people it consumes.' The Earth, the pastor would say, has its mouth wide open ready to receive death's spoils and never takes a break or gets full. To my joy, Pastor Chende was also among the mourners present at the graveyard.

The two graves stood about ten metres apart. Martha's casket was the first to be lowered. My mother-in-law wept in low mournful tones as the casket went slowly down.

After the one for Chola had been lowered, Pastor Matandiko stood up to present a short burial message. He gave the analogy of a farmer who casts seed in the ground and lets it die in order to receive a bountiful harvest. That farmer, Matandiko said, does not plant his seed into the ground mourning all the while. On the contrary, he rejoices at the prospect of the harvest that will come as a result of that seed dying in the ground. 'Today, as we put the bodies of these two loved ones in the ground, let's remember the words of the Apostle Paul when he wrote: "What you sow does not come to life unless it dies. When you sow, you do not plant the body that will be, but just a seed, perhaps of wheat or of something else. But God gives it a body as he has determined." ' (1 Corinthians 15:36-38).

Then, to bid farewell to the departed ones, Matandiko read from the Adventist Church Manual the words that remind man of his origin: 'Earth to earth, and dust to dust,' as soil was scooped on two shovels and thrown down into the two graves containing the caskets. Of the family members, my kids and I were the first to throw the soil down on Martha's casket, then several family members followed suit. After that

The Day My World Caved In.

formality, burial diggers assisted by church members started to bury the dead. Suddenly it became clear that the long nightmare I had endured was not after all a dream; it was real. Unless a miracle took place there, Martha and Chola were gone. Lumps of earth from shovels continued to hit the caskets as we watched in agonising silence and helplessness. I was reminded of an email I had read in the form of a poster. A poster in a graveyard read in Shona, a language spoken in Zimbabwe: *'Ane nharo ngaamuke'* (this statement literally challenges the dead to wake up if they have the strength to do so).

Thank God that Christians don't mourn like those in the world who don't know him. Paul, writing his first letter to the church in Corinth, says:

'Listen, I tell you a mystery: We will not all sleep, but we will all be changed – in a flash, in the twinkling of an eye, at the last trumpet. For the trumpet will sound, the dead will be raised imperishable, and we will be changed. For the perishable must clothe itself with the imperishable, and the mortal with immortality. When the perishable has been clothed with the imperishable, and the mortal with immortality, then the saying that is written will come true: "Death has been swallowed up in victory." "Where, O death, is your victory? Where, O death, is your sting?" ' (15:51-55.) I was also reminded of the words of our Lord Jesus who said: 'I am the resurrection and the life. He who believes in me will live, even though he dies; and whoever lives and believes in me will never die.' (John 11:25, 26.)

It is not over until it is over, the saying goes. Death was smiling at the seemingly victorious capture of God's dear ones. Evil angels might have been standing at a distance celebrating the death of two members of God's Kingdom. Their celebration, however, could not last too long as they heard the beautiful sermon and music coming from God's people. The words in the sermon and songs would remind them of the fate that awaited them. It is not over until it is over. God will have the final say when the battle is over. And victory will be given to God's people as death will be thrown into the lake of fire. As Satan and his angels will be thrown into the lake of fire, God's triumphant people will taunt death and its author Satan in the words of that Shona saying: *'Ane nharo ngaamuke*: Satan and your partner death, if you think you have the might, rescue yourselves from that lake of fire!'

5. Burial Day.

Sweating profusely, their bare legs covered with dust, the grave diggers continued their unenviable task until the two graves lay with their protruding bellies. The one in charge of announcements interrupted the singing, telling the mourners through a megaphone that it was then time for putting flowers on the two graves. I moved from where I was and led my kids in putting flowers on the grave of Martha. Names of family members, friends and colleagues from work were called, then each put flowers on the graves of the departed loved ones.

After that, representatives from the two families were given time to say a few words. My cousin Mwape (this name Mwape is so common in the family) stood and thanked the many people who had assisted in many ways 'to make our mourning lighter'. He was followed by Martha's uncle, Mr Jethro Chabala, who also thanked the people for the support they had given us. Then he said something about his departed niece Martha: 'Many of us,' he said, speaking slowly to ensure every word sank in, 'like to say nice things about dead people, even when we know they were not nice at all. However, all the good things that have been said about this niece of mine who has departed from us are all true.' And the man was right. I could testify, having known Martha intimately for sixteen years, that she was just what many people had said that day: a good lady with a magnetic personality that just drew people to her wherever she went.

Pastor Julian Hibbert, associate secretary of the Adventist Church in the Southern Africa-Indian Ocean Division office, stood and spoke about 'a wonderful friend and colleague we have lost in the person of Martha.' He spoke about her cheerfulness and willingness to help whenever and wherever she could. Then he read a message of condolence from the world leader of the Adventist Church, Pastor Jan Paulsen. His message read in part: 'Dear George. On behalf of the General Conference, I wish to extend to you and the family our sincere sympathy as you have suffered the tragic loss of your dear wife. May the promises of the Earth made new bring you the comfort and encouragement needed at this time.'

Our two friends had gone the way of all the living. For them, time had ceased to move. God alone knew how long the grave would hold them. One thing was clear though: at the time of God's trumpet call they will not wake up thinking that time had passed slowly. It will be as the Bible puts it, 'in the twinkling of an eye', 'in a moment'. Their sleep, no matter how long it will appear to their friends who are alive at Jesus' coming,

The Day My World Caved In.

will appear to them like a sleep of a few seconds. They will not know the agony their deaths brought to their loved ones. In fact, in some cases, they will be shocked to learn they had died.

It was time for us to leave our departed friends. We drove back to the Matandikos' where the funeral had been held. Some friends who had driven from far around the country came to bid us farewell, telling us that they would continue to pray for us. As it was late in the afternoon, a few of them chose to stay for the night and start off the following day.

chapter 6

Family Meeting.

In the evening, my late wife's family and mine convened a meeting. The chairman was Mr Jethro Chabala, Martha's uncle, who had earlier spoken at the graveyard. Mr Chabala is a very pleasant character. Before he retired and went to live in Mansa, he worked as a miner in Mufulira. A fat man who wears a perpetual smile, Mr Chabala is an entertaining conversationalist with a great sense of humour. Being the oldest in his family, he is usually present at big occasions like weddings and funerals, and naturally assumes the position of spokesman. His opinions in family discussions are not only generally respected but often carry the day.

'I want to welcome you all to this meeting,' he began. 'This meeting has been organised in order for our two families to speak together before we separate tomorrow.' It had been decided earlier that our families should move from the Matandikos' house to allow them to start living an ordinary, normal life, now that Martha and Chola had been put to rest. 'Our two families,' Uncle Jethro continued, 'have lived very well. George, the man who has lost a wife, has ceased to be an in-law to me; he has become a friend. I hope that the relationship between us will not end because of what has happened.' He went on to recount other experiences involving collaboration between the two families, and then gave an opportunity to other family members on his side to speak before the ball rolled into our family court. My dad was the first to speak. He, too, thanked the group on the other side for the cordial ties that have existed between the two families. After he had finished, Uncle Jethro asked me to

The Day My World Caved In.

say something too.

I began by reiterating what everyone had said. I then went on to speak about my departed beloved wife Martha. I told the gathering that about two days earlier I had been thinking about the years I had lived with Martha and how sweet they had been. 'I tried hard to find what I could term as her weaknesses in those years,' I said, 'but could find none. The woman was just perfect.' My speech was broken with applause at that point. 'In speaking about Martha being perfect,' I continued, 'I do not mean to say that we did not have disagreements and other such things. What I mean is that I found in her character no negative attitudes that stood out. I often told Martha that I wished our roles would change; that she would be the man, the pastor, and I would be the wife, the pastor's wife. I have no doubt that she would have been a better minister than I am. But I doubt whether I would have been a good pastor's wife either. I thank God for giving me the opportunity to share life with such an incredibly wonderful woman.'

Pardon Mwansa, my friend of long standing, was then given the opportunity to speak: *'Umuchinshi ku chipuna mukwai'* (respect to the chair), he started, as all eyes turned in his direction. 'I realise that this funeral still has many more days to go. From here, we all know that our parents will travel home where many people who could not come for various reasons will have the opportunity to express their condolences. According to tradition, my friend George is also supposed to travel home. As his friend and also an administrator at his workplace, I know that it may not be easy for him to take this trip now. Also because he has to be with his children, one of whom is supposed to be in school now, it will be hard for him to undertake this trip.' Mwansa went on to suggest that in view of the constraints he had mentioned, my trip home be postponed to a future date.

Uncle Jethro's brother, Mr Chongo, then took the floor and also spoke about the beautiful relationship that had existed between the two families. 'In closing the meeting, . . .' Mr Chongo said, but before he could finish his thought, Uncle Jethro interrupted him, saying, 'How can you say, "In closing the meeting . . ." Are you the chairman?' Everyone broke into laughter. Seeing that there were no more significant people to make any contributions, Uncle Jethro, the big man, closed the meeting by thanking Pastor and Mrs Matandiko for offering to host the funeral. 'We

6. Family Meeting.

would like God to bless this couple. There are not many who can do what they have done.'

On Thursday 9 March, the group that came from our office in Harare and many others who had driven from afar left. Relatives from the two families who could not leave because of financial constraints were taken to my brother's house (though at that time he and his wife were still in hospital) with Martha's cousin Joyce. My kids Mwape and Brainerd Mwila went back to Harare in the company of colleagues who had come from the office. As there were still other issues to attend to, I decided to remain in Lusaka with the hope of leaving on the Sunday of the following week. Justin and the Chibendes remained to keep me company.

The Day My World Caved In .

. chapter 7

Details of the Accident .

In the evening of that day, Justin and I went to see my brother and his wife, still in the Intensive Care Unit at the University Teaching Hospital. I had had no opportunity of seeing them because of the constant flow of people to the funeral. We found my brother seated on his bed, talking with his daughter Malita. A stitch on one side of his face and a leg cast with plaster of Paris were the only visible signs that he had been in an accident. He rose from his position, hugged me and expressed his condolences. After telling us how he was doing and the condition of his wife and the driver, he explained how the accident occurred.

'There are a number of versions flying around as to what exactly happened,' he said. 'What I shall tell you is the correct version of what I remember happened.' He went on to narrate the details. He remembered seeing an oncoming vehicle colliding with the side of their vehicle, causing both to tumble and roll. 'I was the first to regain consciousness,' he said. 'I got out of the vehicle and began to call the names of the others. For some minutes no one was answering. I looked on the tarmac and saw Martha lying motionless and immediately knew she had died. Minutes later I heard a groan from my wife. I started helping her out of the mangled vehicle. Chola had also died. Not long afterwards, a reverend travelling to Kasama arrived on the scene. He helped to get the three of us who were still alive to the hospital in Serenje.'

Those who were still alive were he himself, his wife and the driver. With the help of the police in Serenje, he contacted the army commander who

7. Details of the Accident.

quickly made arrangements for the survivors to be flown by a military helicopter back to Lusaka.

A day before that hospital visit, two people who had been to the scene of the accident came to the funeral to express their condolences. Their account of what happened differed in some details from the one my brother gave. They said that they saw only one vehicle at the scene of the accident, the vehicle in which my brother and his team were. Furthermore, they said that the accident occurred about 14km before Serenje town. They were of the view that the driver might simply have lost control, noting that the place where the accident occurred was close to a corner. According to them, there were no other deaths apart from those of my wife and young brother.

Jack, who visited the scene of the accident and saw the mangled vehicle, confirmed that the accident happened before Serenje. He, however, felt that my brother's vehicle might have been hit by a truck with a trailer. 'When you look at the dent on the driver's side, you cannot help but conclude that they were hit by some vehicle, most likely a trailer,' Jack said. My sister in-law, who was involved in the accident, only remembers waking up to the consciousness of pain all over. 'To be honest,' she said from her bed, 'I can't remember what happened.' The driver, who could have assisted in telling what really happened, unfortunately died a week later in the intensive care unit. With Martha and Chola gone, details of what occurred will probably remain a mystery.

On Sabbath a friend of mine, Rose Raelly, invited me to have worship at her house. Justin, Patience, the Chibendes and Rose's mother gathered together and sang. Later, Rose presented a talk. During lunch others joined us: Mabel and Chilunji Ng'andu and son Nzila; Tom and Irvin Ngenda and their children Thabo, Miyanda and Joshua; Larry and Doris Mwinga; Crawford and Kasonde Mwinga and their children Nhimba and Lukonde.

In the afternoon we went back to the Matandikos', where a number of singing groups from around Lusaka came to present a programme. Earlier in the week the director of one of the groups had phoned me, asking whether they could organise a musical programme in memory of the late Martha Mwansa who was a musician in her own right. I had consented, feeling it to be an appropriate way to spend that Sabbath afternoon. The groups that came included '12 Gates', 'Aggellain Singers',

The Day My World Caved In.

'Heritage Brothers', 'Chainama', 'Day Break Singers', among others.

The singing from the groups was so good that it was as though we were already in God's Kingdom. My mind was transported from the sorrows of this life to that heavenly sphere where sorrow does not exist – but it was short-lived.

chapter 8

Empty Home
26 Hiller Rd, Gunhill.

Though I had originally planned to leave on the Sunday, it became impossible to do so owing to the many things that were still undone. We therefore decided to leave for Harare on Monday, the following day. By 11 o'clock on Monday, though we had not tied up all loose ends, we decided to start off for Harare. I was worried that if we delayed further we would reach Harare quite late at night. I did not particularly fancy the idea of driving at night. Those who travelled with me were John, my brother-in-law; Mrs Ruth Mofya, my mother-in-law; Mrs Loveness Besa, my sister-in-law; and her daughter Besa. We travelled without incident and arrived in Harare at about 7:30. Earlier, my friend Pardon had called to tell us to go to his house upon arrival. We thanked God for a safe trip. My kids and my friends Judy and Pardon, who had been eagerly waiting for us that day, showered each one of us with hugs and helped to remove our things from the car. After we had rested for a few minutes, Judy invited us to the table for supper. Mrs Denise Ratsara, a colleague at work and friend of Martha, had prepared that evening's meal for us. She had learned of our coming and had offered to help prepare the meal. It was good to know that friends were thinking about us in such a practical way.

The kids looked all right. Mwape, the quiet girl who has taken so much after me in character, was there with her usual calm and collected manner. Brainerd Mwila, too, was just his usual self. I reasoned that as they were still so young, the impact of the loss of their mother had not yet fully registered; after all, they hadn't yet moved to our house in

The Day My World Caved In.

Gunhill. For a while, I thought about the future that awaited them. I wondered just how their lives would evolve without their mother. Whichever way one viewed the matter, growing up without a mother is fraught more with disadvantages than advantages. In fact, I cannot think of any advantages of growing up without a mother. However, as a Christian, I believe that in everything God works for the good of those who love him. Some occurrences are good while others are bad. However, good or bad, God can use them to the advantage and good of his people.

It was Judy and Pardon's view that we spend that night at their house and move home the following day. We had no objections to that. The following day around mid-morning, we left, in the company of Pardon, for our home in Gunhill. I pondered what it would be like to enter that house – no more to be welcomed by Martha.

There was another painful moment when our vehicle pulled up outside our gate and our gardener Matheus opened it as we drove through. Tears in his eyes, Matheus came to greet us and help get our luggage from the vehicle. There is no doubt that Matheus, like all of us, had been shaken. This is the man who has been working for us since 1996 when we came to Harare. Then we were staying at 17 Somerset Drive in Eastlea. At that time Matheus was just a single young man. Now married with a child and his wife expecting another, Matheus was more than just our worker. He was a family member. Having closely worked with my wife, who was his immediate supervisor, Matheus undoubtedly felt the loss just as keenly.

Moving from the car, I proceeded to the front door with the key in my right hand. I inserted the key into the hole, and as it turned my heart missed a beat. Before I could open the door, I wondered what it was going to be like stepping into that empty house. Finally I took the dreaded step as my eyes gave one sweeping look at the things inside that room. The books on the shelves, sofas, hi-fi-system, television and whatever else was there – all were intact. But something big was missing. This was no longer the happy, lovely and bubbly home we had become used to. A home is not made up of the things that are bought from outside and placed there. Rather, it is made up of the love that abides. And Martha had been the cornerstone of that love. She made all of us feel so welcome that it was just a joy to live in that house. Now, the big-hearted woman who had provided that love and shaped the life and activities of that home was gone – never again to be seen this side of

8. Empty Home 26 Hiller Rd, Gunhill.

eternity. What, I asked myself, would become of house number 26 along Hiller Road in Gunhill?

When I entered the living room, my eyes went straight to the section above the fireplace where our large family portrait hangs. I noticed that it had been taken down. I remembered how my mother-in-law wept as she sat in the church at Libala during the funeral service. On Martha's casket directly in front of my mother-in-law's seat, was Martha's beautiful portrait. Wearing a beautiful smile, she was looking gorgeous. In the middle of the sermon I saw my mother-in-law leave her seat and go outside. Later, an elder came and whispered to me that she was having trouble looking at the portrait of her daughter and was asking if it could be removed. Minutes after the portrait was removed we saw her enter the church and take her seat. Perhaps remembering this incident, Judy, who had come earlier that morning to the house, might have removed the portrait. That family portrait and the one of Martha had been removed, creating an uneasy imbalance in way the photos were arranged. My portrait and that of my kids were the only pictures that greeted us as we entered the living room. I was once again reminded of the grim realities of loss through death.

From the living-room I proceeded to the main bedroom, the room where Martha and I had shared our unified but now disrupted life together. I sat down on a lifeless bed that rested firmly on a thinly carpeted floor, a bed covered with a brightly coloured bedspread. Resting there, I brooded over my fate. Items in the room kept staring me in the face, making me wonder why I had to endure such grief at that time. The sound of the clock on the wall kept interrupting the strange silence in the room, reminding me that life had to continue, despite what had happened. I sat there lost in thoughts God alone can understand. Surely, God in his infinite wisdom could have simply created us without the possibility of disobeying him, disobedience that had led to our messed-up lives. Or maybe God could have simply created me to be like one of those angels who never followed Satan into rebellion. How different life would have been! I could now be somewhere in Heaven just enjoying life with God. Engrossed in wishful thinking, my mind was oblivious to the immediate surroundings. But that ticking clock kept reviving me from the harsh stupor, reminding me time and again that the wheels of time had to continue grinding on in the harsh manner to which we are accustomed.

The Day My World Caved In.

I stood up and moved to the closet that contained Martha's dresses. My eyes were greeted by empty hangers. The clothes had been removed that morning before we came to the house. Bemba tradition demands that when a woman dies all her dresses should be taken by her relatives. I personally had no problem with this view, for what would the husband do with the dresses? Early that morning, Judy had escorted my sister-in-law Loveness to my house to remove all the dresses and shoes and put them in suitcases. There was no foul play there. The suitcases were left in the bedroom for me to inspect and ensure that what had been taken had belonged to Martha.

In the meantime, news had quickly circulated in town that we had arrived. Those who could make it that morning came to offer their condolences. By evening it appeared everyone from our church at Highlands had learned of our arrival. Outside and inside our yard vehicles parked. The living, dining and TV rooms were all filled with people. Pastor Zacheaus Mathema, a colleague from the office, shared that evening's message with us. At the end of that service, it was announced that that week up to Friday there would be evening services at our house. Members were urged to keep coming as a way of showing us support. People trooped in numbers all week. Some of the ladies brought food and helped prepare it. From the show of sympathy and support, one could tell that Martha had touched many lives at church and beyond. She had built for herself a good name through her kind deeds and participation in church activities. People came not so much because she was Pastor George Mwansa's wife but because of her own positive impact at church, at the workplace and beyond. She had not lived her life in the shadow of George Mwansa. She was her own woman. Her life was a powerful testimony that no matter what our station in life might be, we can all live our lives and leave our own imprint on planet Earth. As a pastor's wife, it was easy for Martha to be seen always through the connection she had with me. The servant leadership modelled by Jesus notwithstanding, the pastor's position is apt to tower high and recognise only one person – the pastor. But Martha walked the Earth with her Saviour, wrote and left her own history. She lived as Martha and went as Martha.

As the time came to go to bed that evening, I contemplated the prospect of sleeping alone. Night's dark shadows have a way of playing devastating havoc on the emotions. The fear of the unknown often takes

8. Empty Home 26 Hiller Rd, Gunhill.

over at night and causes even educated people to lose their sanity. I read of a youngster who prayed only at night. When asked why he did not pray in the morning, he said, 'Because I am only afraid at night.' An empty pillow on Martha's side stared at me. A couple of books she must have been reading lay on the bedside cabinet. I reminded myself of Jesus' promise to be with his people till the end of time and imagined him sleeping right next to me. I could hear him saying to me: 'I will never leave you nor forsake you.' How comforting the thought! Then I remembered the many times Martha woke me up from some terrible nightmares. There was one, for example, on the night of 25 December 2004. I had found myself in a terrible struggle to breathe. It was as if a powerful force was trying to choke the life out of me. I gathered all the strength I could muster in a desperate life-and-death struggle to free myself from the mysterious tyrannical power, but failed to release myself from the grip. I was by then partly conscious of the fact that my time to go the way of all the living had come. I put up a hard fight but seemed to lose it. Then I felt a hand pushing me. Martha, faithful to that task, was at it once again. The push continued for a little while before I finally woke up from that nightmare. I don't remember having a nightmare as bad as that in a long time.

I also have this habit sometimes of sleeping on my back. Often when I sleep like that I have nightmares. My brain doesn't like my sleeping in that position. Martha was always there to wake me up from such nightmares. I asked myself what would happen if I had one of those bad dreams. Who would be there to wake me up? I heard a whisper in my mind. Christ was saying: 'Remember, even when Martha was asleep, I was still awake. Don't worry. I am going to help you.' With that comforting thought, I went to sleep. Soon I lost consciousness and drifted into the land of dreams. Moments later, I woke up with a desperate gasp for air. 'Oh, no,' I said, 'it can't be those nightmares again!' I reminded my Lord Jesus about his assurance to be with me and help me during nightmares. I prayed once again for God's protection and authority over me and immediately fell asleep. The next time I opened my eyes the night had long gone and broken into morning. I woke up to the empty feeling of Martha's absence. For a time I just lay on the bed, staring into space.

The days and weeks that followed were, as all might expect, difficult ones. Whether I was at home or wherever I happened to be, the death of

The Day My World Caved In.

my wife constantly kept playing itself before me. Often I would imagine the ordeal my dear wife went through before she finally took her last breath. Always that thought had a crushing effect upon me. At times I thought of the moment I was told at the hospital that Martha had died on the spot. Reliving that experience was always emotionally draining and painful.

Then came times when I thought about the agony of remarriage. Surely, at my age, trying to make new relationships – new in-laws and all the new people from the family of the wife that I had to know and get used to – did not seem an attractive prospect. I hated the thought of having babies and changing nappies again. I imagined the constant interrupted sleep I would have to go through again from the incessant crying. Surely, God knew how I hated going through that experience and he would save me from it. Mwape, my first-born child, always wanted to sleep with the lights on when she was born. I hated that ordeal because I found it so hard to sleep. I thought of sleeping with the lights on again to accommodate the babies of a new marriage, and, frankly, felt mad with God.

Each time I saw my kids, I felt like crying. I wondered how life was going to be for them growing up without a mother. Would someone out there in the Christian community offer herself as mother to the children, especially Mwape, the girl?

One day my son told me something which he heard from Uncle Pardon: 'You know, Dad, Uncle Pardon one day told me that when he was a kid he used to hear preachers talk about Jesus coming soon. But Jesus hasn't come yet. Uncle Pardon is an old man with a family. Is Jesus really coming soon? I hope Jesus will come soon because I want to see my mum soon. I don't want to grow old and have a family of my own.' I had no words for my son because I didn't know when Christ was coming. At another time my son came to share what was on his mind: 'Dad, I have thought about following you to your concerts so that I could also play some songs, but now that Mum is dead, are we ever going to be singing again?' I assured him that we would continue to sing, despite what had happened. 'But, Dad,' he asked, 'are we going to find someone to replace Mum?' 'We will have to,' I told him. 'Anyway, I just don't think she will be as good as Mum. Maybe I'm just saying this because she was my mum.'

chapter 9

'Cleansing' --
Isambwe lyamfwa.

A month later, I asked for compassionate leave at my workplace in order to travel to Mansa, Zambia, for what's called *isambwe lyamfwa*. In my culture, when a spouse dies, a meeting of key relatives from both parties takes place to look at a number of issues like how property will be divided and whether the surviving spouse would like to be given a woman from the family of the deceased, if one is available. But that aside, it is believed that when one's spouse dies, the dead one turns into a ghost and literally clings to the surviving spouse until the dead spouse is 'cleansed'. There are different ways of 'cleansing'. One such form is to sleep with a woman provided by the relatives of the dead person. The cleansing of the ghost takes place that way and releases the survivor to go on with life and even marry if he or she so chooses. So the trip was more than just about relatives from my side and those of my late wife Martha meeting, but was intended for this ritual to take place as well. Of course, as a Christian, I don't share in such beliefs, and therefore did not expect this aspect to be part of what I was going to be subjected to. I made this clear to my relatives, as some of them anticipated this ceremony.

My good friend Pardon decided to travel with me and provide any help I needed. We started off on a Thursday for Lusaka and spent the night there. The following day we left for Mansa, a distance of 800km. Pardon had received information about the area near Serenje where Martha had been killed. About 400km from Lusaka as we neared Serenje, he noticed a place close to the scene of the accident and began to slow down.

The Day My World Caved In.

Somewhere on a straight stretch, driving slowly, we saw dark marks of spilled oil and we stopped. I told Pardon that that could not be the location, as we had been told that it was near a corner. Pardon got out of the vehicle and went to check the area and confirmed that he was right. I disputed further, arguing once again that the place had been near a corner. My sister-in-law Mary, who had joined us in Lusaka, and I also left the vehicle and went to join Pardon. Nearby, at the side of the road was a concrete milestone that was slanting leftward, giving an indication of having been hit by a strong object. We agreed that an accident might have taken place there but not necessarily the one in which Martha had died. There were also pieces of broken glass and other items that might have broken off from a crashing vehicle. I noticed in the nearby bush a piece of newspaper. I picked it up and noticed it was *The Post*, a popular Zambian tabloid. A check on the date revealed Saturday 5 March. The accident had taken place on Sunday 6 March. I reasoned that since Martha's crew had left very early Sunday morning, the only newspaper they could have carried with them was probably Saturday's.

Pardon remained convinced that he was right. 'I was given the name of a particular school on our right and a small village about a kilometre before this place,' Pardon said, 'and was told to begin looking for this spot. I think this must be the place.' We then started looking for anything that could give further evidence that that assumption was correct. I spotted in the nearby grass an abandoned drinking glass. 'This glass looks like those we have at home,' I reported to the others. They each looked at it as I asked Mary to keep it so we could carry it with us. As we were trying to put pieces together, we saw three people coming from the direction of the village we had left about a kilometre from that spot. When they arrived, we asked if they knew anything about an accident that had occurred in the vicinity not too long before. They said they had heard about it and confirmed that it happened right on the spot where we were. 'Though we cannot provide the details since we don't live here,' one of them said, 'we know it was here.' We asked if they could provide any other details they could remember. One of them said that the accident had happened on a Sunday and two people, a man and a woman, had been killed on the spot. We then concluded this was indeed the spot. Having established this truth, we then wanted to know just how the accident happened. We had expected to see skid marks from sudden

9. 'Cleansing' -- *Isambwe lyamfwa*.

braking, but saw nothing on the scene. However, about twenty or so metres away, we noticed some slightly faded tyre marks. The marks first appeared turning to the left side and then there was an extreme turn to the right. (In Zambia we drive on the left side of the road.) The marks on the left were more pronounced than on the right. We pondered over what exactly had happened. We asked why the driver had moved the vehicle to the left, almost leaving the road, and then suddenly swung to the right.

One view we came up with was that in the event of an approaching vehicle taking up too much of the space on the left, the driver of my wife's group might have swung to the left to avoid a head-on collision. But then why swing suddenly to the extreme right? It did not make traffic sense that the driver in trying to avoid a collision with an oncoming vehicle would immediately swing to the right. It appeared more reasonable to think that the driver and indeed all the others in the vehicle except Martha might have been dozing. My elder brother had said that he had heard Martha shout the driver's name just before the accident happened. That might have been to alert him that he was coming off the road. The driver, waking up from that short nap, panicked and immediately tried to bring the vehicle back onto the road. But he did it so sharply that the vehicle lost balance, tumbled and rolled. We could not tell how many times it rolled, but as it crossed to the other side it hit the concrete milepost and pavement. It seemed to us that that was what had happened. Initial reports from some of those who had been to the scene of the accident indicated that the accident happened near a corner. However, that was not true. The stretch where the accident took place was so straight and so long that one could drive up to speeds of even 200km an hour.

We spent about thirty minutes there, just trying to reconstruct what could have happened. It was obviously another sad moment for me. I had been told that Martha had been thrown out of the vehicle and her body for some time just lay on the tarmac, waiting to be taken by police to the mortuary in Serenje. I pictured the gruesome scene in my mind. After taking several shots of the accident scene with my digital camera, we started off for Serenje, sixteen kilometres away.

In Serenje, we stopped to buy fuel at the filling station close to the main road. We asked a young petrol attendant if she remembered an accident in which two people had been killed about a month before. She

The Day My World Caved In.

confirmed she had. She told us that on that fateful Sunday she had been working in the morning and that the accident had happened around 11am. The young lady said that we could get more information at the local police station not far from where we were.

There we found a young police officer who recognised me from my music videos on national television. Pardon introduced the subject and told her we just wanted to have an idea of what happened. The policewoman called a male colleague, who had been to the scene of the accident, to help furnish details. The officer told us what he could remember. 'The body of the woman was lying on the tarmac while that of the man was off the road, close to where the vehicle had stopped.' He told us that we could get more information from an officer manning the roadblock on the highway. 'You will find an officer on your way who visited the scene earlier than I did and drew a sketch of what happened. He will be able to furnish more details.' Unfortunately, when we got to the roadblock that police officer had left. However, the one who was there told us the bits he remembered. We asked him what he thought caused the accident and he said something close to what we suspected. 'My impression is that the driver was tired and dozing.' He flatly denied that another vehicle had been involved.

We reached Mansa on the Friday and on the Sabbath rested according to our custom. Sunday was the big day for that important meeting. Before our group left, I had a private discussion with my father, in which I asked him about what really took place at such meetings and what code of conduct was expected of me as a widower. Dad told me that a few metres away from the house of Mr Jethro Chabala, where the meeting was to take place, all the ladies accompanying us 'must begin to cry'. I didn't understand the meaning of such a weird custom, but I didn't care to ask why that had to be done. 'Upon arrival, the other party will then receive us and show us where to sit. You as the widower are not expected to sit on a chair; you must sit on the ground,' Dad said.

My young brother Mwelwa helped to ferry a few of my aunties from Chofoshi village to Martha's uncle's, about 12km from the town centre, while I took my dad and a few other VIP's from our group. Just as my dad had said, upon arrival, the ladies grouped themselves together and started crying as they began to approach the house of Mr Jethro Chabala, Martha's uncle. No sooner had they started crying than Mr Chabala from

9. 'Cleansing' -- *Isambwe lyamfwa*.

where he stood commanded them to stop crying. 'We are not here to start mourning but to talk. I don't want you to start crying.' The ladies resisted the call for a few minutes, but the man insisted, and finally they stopped crying.

The meeting opened with Mr Chabala thanking our group for showing up for the meeting, 'though you are late.' He then went on to speak at length about the beautiful life that his niece, Martha, had lived. 'She was simply the best. There is no one in the family that I can compare her with. Her death has saddened us.' Before we could come to the main issue, I was given an opportunity to say something. I talked about the beautiful life I had enjoyed with my late wife Martha. I told the gathering that Martha had been a lady any man could be proud of. 'Martha had no flaws,' I said. 'In the sixteen years we lived together I never detected any flaws in her life. She was simply perfect. Not perfect in the sense of not being capable of making mistakes. Rather, perfect in the sense that there was not a single negative trait that stood out in her life. Like every human being she made mistakes, but these were rare.' I then thanked my mother-in-law and other members of Martha's family for bringing her up so well. When I stopped speaking, my cousin Paul asked if he could say something. Paul went on to speak about Martha as 'simply the best woman one could come across.' My aunt Delphine (bana Mwengwe for those who don't recognise that name) spoke in glowing terms of Martha's life: 'I feel very sorry for you, my son, as I don't think you will ever find a woman as good as Martha in this world.' Others followed suit and spoke about the wonderful person Martha had been.

Finally, the big question that everyone was waiting for was asked. With all the tact he could muster and not beating about the bush, the big man Mr Chabala asked me whether I would want to be given a woman from the family or not. That was a question I had taken time to reflect on. I had gone round in circles, thinking of who could replace Martha from their family. In the immediate family, there was only Mary, the youngest among the girls. Mary had become almost a child to us, having lived with us for some time at 17 Somerset Drive in Eastlea. She had come to do a secretarial course at one of the colleges in Harare. Though she was old enough to assume the role the sister had left prematurely, there was a sense in which the whole idea appeared unpalatable. I was used to calling Mary my little sister and could she now become my wife? Mary by nature

The Day My World Caved In.

is quiet. She usually talks only in the company of those she knows well. Would she rise to the rigorous demands of a pastor's wife? True, the kids would perhaps adjust to Auntie Mary as the new mother more easily than to any other person. But the role of a pastor's wife is challenging and needs the blessing of God to work successfully.

I needed to know my actions would be in accordance with God's will. Moreover, at that time Mary was going out with another guy in a very steady relationship. I didn't feel it would be prudent to take someone's lady on the strength of tradition. And what if Mary herself was not interested and was simply forced to play the game and obey the rules? After carefully weighing the matter, I had concluded that even if Mary was the right person I could not simply accept a woman right then. The wounds from my wife's death were still very fresh. I needed time to heal before I could even begin to entertain the idea of marrying again.

'Right now,' I said, 'I am not in a position to say anything on this matter because I am still mourning the death of my wife. I would like to be given time to heal. Moreover, the position of the wife of a pastor is so crucial and so demanding that I would not want to go into another relationship without knowing that God was leading me. I therefore need time to reflect. At the right time, I will come back and tell this assembly my thoughts.' People from my mother-in-law's side responded with applause. 'Thank you,' my mother-in-law said.

After that meeting my friend Pardon stayed for a day or two before he left on a bus for Lusaka. Since I still had some days left of my compassionate leave, I decided to take advantage of that time by visiting many of my relatives who had not made it to the funeral.

Finally the day of departure for Lusaka came. On this trip Loveness, Mary and Richard Chongo – a friend of mine – and I started off for the more-than-700km trip to Lusaka very early in the morning. We got to Serenje at about ten o'clock in the morning and drove to the police station to get the report on the accident. I introduced myself and went straight to the reason I was there. I was told that the policeman who had visited the scene of the accident was not at the station. I was promised that the report would be written as soon as he returned. I left my contact details and some money for the report to be sent by the fastest means. Sixteen kilometres beyond Serenje we were back at the scene of the accident. I parked the vehicle by the side of the road as I showed

9. 'Cleansing' -- *Isambwe lyamfwa*.

Loveness and Richard where the deaths had occurred. That spot, as far as I am concerned, is the blackest in the entire country of Zambia, for that is where the precious life of my dear wife Martha was claimed. Again I began to picture what my dear ones must have gone through at the moment when the vehicle overturned. I looked at the spot on the tarmac where it was said Martha lay dead, having been thrown out of the vehicle. My dear one whose only mission had been to go and mourn her sister-in-law, who had passed away earlier in the week, had herself met a tragic end at that black spot. How could life be so cruel?

As we stood there trying to put the pieces of that accident together, several men walking from some village stopped and greeted us. We asked if they remembered an accident that happened there a few weeks earlier. 'The man who was among the first to arrive on the scene,' stated one man, 'lives not far from here. The people who died in that accident were, actually, hit by a truck. The truck driver had stopped after seeing what happened but later drove off. A certain woman, who had been driving from somewhere and was one of those who arrived first on the scene, sped off after the truck driver and confronted him at a police roadblock not far from here. That truck driver was detained but later released.'

Obviously, that information was new to us. I asked whom we could approach to get more information. The man told us to ask the police at the roadblock a few kilometres ahead of us. I tried to put the pieces together again and reconstruct what could have happened. 'Maybe what could have happened,' I said to the others, 'is that the driver swung to the left when he saw that the oncoming truck was going to hit him, and in a bid to avoid going into the bush he made another sharp swing to the right, causing the vehicle to overturn.' But then again, I thought, why didn't the police say that? According to their report given verbally, there was nothing to suggest that another vehicle had been involved. Moreover, the fact that the marks of the tyres on the tarmac had shown a sudden turn to the left and an equally sudden turn to the right and the fact that the vehicle overturned and stopped on the right-hand side of the road did not suggest the involvement of another vehicle.

As we pulled away from the scene of the accident, the subject of what could have happened dominated the conversation. We drove for quite a distance before we came to the police roadblock. I stopped the car and went to park by the roadside. I went to where the policemen stood and

The Day My World Caved In.

asked whether they remembered an accident that took place near Serenje on 6 March. They said they did not. 'On the said date,' said one officer, 'the ones that were manning this roadblock were from Serenje and we ourselves are from Mkushi.' I thanked them and left to join the others in the car. I drove in silence, wondering just who would be able to explain what had happened.

    In the evening of that same day after our arrival in Lusaka, Loveness and I went to see my elder brother and his wife at their home along Independence Avenue. My brother sat in the living room with – I suppose – friends from his workplace. After exchanging greetings with my brother and his friends, we proceeded to the TV room where my brother's wife Catherine sat warming herself with a heater as she watched TV. Her face appeared sombre. One could tell that the shock of that traumatic moment still affected her. I went on to give her a detailed account of how we had travelled and said that I had taken some pictures of the scene of the accident which I had loaded on my laptop. At some point when my brother joined us, I took the laptop from the bag and showed them the pictures. I went on to explain my own reconstruction of the accident, based on what I had observed. I told them that I had the impression that their driver had begun to doze and the vehicle was about to stray into the bush to the left when Martha shouted from behind, alerting the driver that they were veering off into the bush. Waking from his brief nap and obviously panic-stricken, the driver swung the vehicle immediately to his right, resulting in its overturning and crossing to the other side of the road.

    I showed them the marks of the skidding tyres which were visible even on the picture. My brother still objected to that reconstruction. 'I remember seeing a small vehicle coming in front and moving as if about to hit us,' my brother countered. 'It was at that point that your wife shouted the driver's name from behind where she sat. She shouted apparently to warn him of that approaching vehicle. We were later told that even in that other vehicle some people had also died.' I told my brother that, according to the account given by the police, there was no other vehicle involved, and that as a matter of fact the only people who died were those in their car. My brother was also of the opinion that the accident took place after Serenje, yet it occurred about 16km before Serenje, if one was coming from Lusaka. Fortunately, because I had

9. 'Cleansing' -- *Isambwe lyamfwa* .

pictures, it was not hard to convince him on that point. I finally concluded that what took place on that fateful Sunday of 6 March will be known only in eternity. Had Martha survived, she could have told us what happened because she was awake. Unfortunately, Catherine was fast asleep and so she couldn't remember what happened. The talk of the accident and pictures from the scene did not go down well with Catherine. It was like reliving the whole episode. She broke down and refused to be comforted.

The Day My World Caved In.

chapter 10

Painful Recollections.

Life after the death of a loved one takes a very lonely path. A few weeks after coming back to Harare, I escorted a friend to a mall. I told her that I would remain in the vehicle while she went to buy some items. While she was gone, I began to play on the car's radio a tape recorded by the Maranatha Singers of the USA. One song reminded me of Martha. Tears began to flow freely as I prayed that God would delay the coming of my friend so she would not find me crying. God answered that prayer. Like a little child, I just let tears flow, at the same time praying that no one would pass by. Why, I asked, did God allow such a good person to die? When I saw my friend coming in the distance, I quickly wiped my tears and pretended that all was well.

Another time I happened to be in Kitwe, Zambia. That evening I decided to go and see Bodwin and Alice Chishimba, good friends of mine who lived in Riverside. As I drove to their house, that same music from the Maranatha Singers was playing on tape. Suddenly, without warning, I felt a sweep of emotion engulf me. Martha's sweet personality and life seemed to pass before my mind's eye. As her life replayed itself, my own emerged from its hiding place and stood comparing itself with hers. I saw myself as a failure. True, I was a pastor, but I could not compare my filthy life with hers. Tears began to flow. In my sobs, I prayed that God would help me to become like Martha. I stopped the vehicle and parked by some shopping complex not far from my friends' house. I cried over the fact that I was such a great sinner. I pleaded with God to have mercy on me. I

10. Painful Recollections

told God over and over again that I wanted to live like my late wife. No matter how hard I tried to control it, the river of tears continued to flow with unabated force. For over an hour I just sat in the car, crying like a little girl who had lost her prized doll. When the pent-up emotion had waned, I started off slowly for the Chishimbas'. When I arrived at the gate, I checked the mirror in the car to make sure my tear-stained face was dry before I honked for the guard to open the gate for me.

I cannot remember how many times I sat in my bedroom at home overwhelmed by something and just cried. Sometimes it would be a simple thing like failing to locate an item in the bedroom. At other times it would be just the loneliness of living alone with no helpmate. I would sit and simply cry. I would always make sure the room was locked so the kids did not walk in suddenly. Sometimes I would feel sorry for them that they had lost a mother at a time they needed her most. One Sabbath, I accompanied my son to Border Adventist church where he was participating in a music programme. He had been asked to play several piano pieces as well as a violin performance with Mrs Bekker at the piano. As he stood to play the duet with Mrs Bekker, my heart missed a few beats. I just wasn't sure he would be able to play the violin well in front of so many people. The young man rose to the occasion and gave a good account of himself. I felt proud. But I also felt sad. I felt sad that his mother had not been there to witness what her young son was slowly becoming – an accomplished musician. Had I been alone in that church I am sure I would have shed tears. The death of a spouse is painful and can disorient a person quite badly. There were times I had no strength to pray. I just watched life in silent resignation. I thank God that so many people were praying for the children and me.

The company of Chisha, Besa and John at home did a lot to help. Those were the people who were there with us up to the time Martha passed away. They helped with household chores and made life a little more worth living. However, because they were young, they often didn't include me in their activities. I thus felt lonely quite often. Usually at mealtimes they would eat in the TV room, leaving me alone at the table. Here I have to commend my son, Mwila, for sticking with me in that situation. As others would take their plates (this included my daughter Mwape as well), Mwila would stay at the table and eat with me. Mwila also liked to sleep in my bedroom, even though he didn't derive much fun

The Day My World Caved In.

from that exercise. He was always thinking of how he could help reduce Dad's loneliness. On the whole, the guys at home played a very important role in helping me to cope with the loss of my wife. Of course, each one of them was also struggling to cope in his or her own way.

The death of their mother was a tricky subject of conversation with the kids but, nevertheless, had to be tackled sometimes. I often discussed it from the standpoint of the resurrection. The kids agreed that their mother was a nice and loving person and that one day they would see her. 'Death is tricky,' I told the kids one day. 'Do you know that your mother doesn't even know that she is dead?' 'What do you mean, Dad,' my son queried. 'Well, when life goes out you lose consciousness. It's like being in a dreamless sleep. You guys have experienced times when after waking you virtually can't remember a thing. When your mother wakes up on the resurrection morning, she will be surprised to learn that she'd been actually dead,' I said. 'I guess you are right, Dad,' Mwila said, 'but when I see her laughing, I will say, "Mum, you put us through so much pain."'

One time my son came to talk to me. 'Dad, you know Mwape and I think that you shouldn't marry again. We talked about it the other day.' I told him that I could not make a comment then as we had a long future ahead of us. 'We must learn to live just one day at a time. God in his own time will reveal to us what to do,' I said. At one time he came to ask me how God could be a loving Father 'when he takes away your mother.' I don't remember how I answered him.

A few weeks after we came back from the funeral in Lusaka, I went to my computer to try to edit the videos we had recorded while Martha was still alive. I looked at the image of Martha in one of the videos and just felt I wasn't ready to do that work. She had that serene look that just made me miss her so much. A couple of weeks later, I decided to go back to the computer and start the editing process. I used as many good shots as I could find of Martha, knowing that that was the last video album in which she was going to appear. The more I saw the images, the more I got used to working with the materials. It was actually providential that she featured in the new video album, as I had written most of the songs we did. The album is titled 'Songs From the Heart'. It is a collection of some of the songs people have liked from the albums I did from 1997-2004.

chapter 11

Back at the Office

At my workplace, there were those who were always ready to help. I think of Mrs Chisewe who would privately send us food at home. She did not want us to know, but the friend who was bringing the food betrayed her. She told me that she just didn't feel it fair for me to think she was the one giving the stuff when it was Mrs Chisewe. 'You could end up thinking I am the holy woman doing this,' her friend said. Mrs Alice Mafanuke offered a lot of prayers and often checked on the kids at home to see how everyone was doing and how we were running on supplies. She helped with Mwape's school preparations as well. That was especially after Mrs Judith Mwansa left. Mrs Nelly Llaguno often picked the kids up for meals. Her bubbly personality was always apparent and was very much appreciated. Mrs and Mr Bekker often brought us cakes and other eats. They visited to check on us and to pray for us. Mrs Patience Shumba acted as the 'good sister'. She would often tell me to feel free to say whatever I needed so she could help. Her kids, Miranda and Nyasha, provided plenty of fun. We often ate at the Shumbas'. Mrs Esther Moyo often popped by the office to check on how I was doing. Mrs Maria Mutseriwa helped with what little allowances I was entitled to and made sure that she prepared the papers that entitled me to get the money. She visited and prayed for me on a number of occasions. Alice Mafanuke and Ruthy Nyawasha were also very helpful in the matter of allowances that were due to me. Sister Christine Johns was always good with her greetings, although she often bothered me about my music. Mrs Judy

The Day My World Caved In.

Mwansa was everything. She counted it her duty to help in every way. Mrs Shingi Janda was good at providing help in matters related to her work and very often invited us for meals at her house.

Of course, going back to the office wasn't easy. I think of the first day I went into the worship room after the death of Martha. We had always occupied the front seats. I dreaded the moment. I was tempted not to sit in the usual place in order not to attract the attention of the people. But I decided to put on a brave face and walked all the way to the front and took my seat. Martha's seat was conspicuously empty! Because I sat right in front, I imagined all the faces behind looking at me and quite honestly felt uneasy and insecure.

The other place I avoided entering as much as I could was the insurance office that Martha had occupied before she died. The new person, Ruthy Nyawasha, had called me one day so we could sort out Martha's insurance claim. I had managed to obtain the police report and the death certificate that she needed in order to process the claim. The first thing Ruthy did when I entered the office was to give me Martha's personal items. I sat in that office brooding over life's incomprehensible twists. Not too long before, Martha had been working in that office doing what Ruthy was then doing. The one who used to process insurance claims was gone. It was time for her own claims to be attended to by someone else. Who would have thought that such a thing would occur so suddenly? I looked at the chair where Martha used to sit, then occupied by our friend Ruthy, who had previously served as transportation officer. The big table and some other items lay as they had been before, with the exception of a few changes. I handed the police report and the death certificate to Ruthy, and in turn she gave me an insurance claim form which she helped me to fill.

On 30 May, my birthday, almost the entire office surprised me by coming to my office to sing the 'Happy Birthday to You' song. Each one came with an egg that he or she left with me in the office. Up to today I do not understand the significance of those eggs. I mean, why they chose eggs in particular, I don't know. I can only speculate that the egg game was conceived in the mind of Mr Jannie Bekker, the humorous Southern Africa-Indian Ocean Division man.

At one time, I did something at the office that brought tears to some people's eyes. During worship I showed a video I had edited that showed

11. Back at the Office.

'live' pictures of Martha and me at the camp meeting for professionals and business people that was held at the St George's Hotel in Pretoria. To many, Martha's picture was just too real to be shown so early. Had I known that it would evoke such depressing emotions, I would never have shown it. I am sorry, guys, for showing you that video!

In my office, I often sat lost in my own fractured world. I would do one or two things absent-mindedly before retiring home, where the situation did not help much. I was overwhelmed by the many emails of condolence that I received. I must admit that I had no strength to reply to many of them. Some came from individuals while others were from organisations. I shall give a sample of a few here.

Elder Bekele Biri, former executive secretary of the Eastern Africa Division, wrote: 'Dear Brother Mwansa. My wife and I have just received the shocking news of the passing away of your dear wife, indeed, our dear daughter. We are so profoundly shaken that we just do not know what to say. We do not understand why a young mother had to be cut short when older ones continue.'

Mr George Egwakhe, treasurer of the Southern Asia-Pacific Division, who had, himself, lost a son in an accident on the basketball court not too long previously, wrote assuring me of his prayers for me. 'Remember,' he wrote, 'there is nothing one can do to bring them back, and you need to be alive to support your children.'

Writing on behalf of the Trans-European Division, executive secretary Harald Wollan, wrote: 'The sad news of the tragic accident has just reached me, and my heart goes out to you and your children for the heartbreaking loss of your wife. I know that words cannot describe the grief you are going through, and it is difficult to put something in writing that could be of comfort in times of loss, but we would like you to know that you are in our thoughts and prayers.'

Dr John Kakembo, executive secretary of the Adventist Church in Uganda, was at a loss for words. He wrote: 'Dear George. It was with unspeakable grief that I learnt about the unspeakable tragedy. I honestly have no words for you. I will only pray for you now.'

Pastor Francois Louw, president of the Adventist Church in the Cape Conference, wrote about the 'great shock and sadness that we have received on hearing this very bad news.'

Brother Mwanahiba, associate treasurer of the Adventist Church in

The Day My World Caved In.

Mozambique, in his letter of condolence to Dr Pardon Mwansa, leader of the Adventist Church in the Southern Africa-Indian Ocean Division, could not understand how 'the man can cope with this, honestly.'

My good friend Rhoda Nthani wrote: 'While it may seem awkward to say so, I do give thanks to God even in this loss. Martha has been a testimony of how we should live as children of God. Of all our friends and contacts that I have made in my life, Martha was the jewel I could look to for an example of what it means to be a child of God. The way she spent her time, took care of her home, took care of others and the way she took care of her husband and praised him, Martha was unique. I know that you know all this, but I just wanted to express thanks for the example she led and above all thank God for her being a testimony to us all.'

There were, indeed, many who wrote emails and letters, and still others who phoned, offering encouragement and promises to pray for the children and me. The list is so long that I can give only a sample of what I received. Some of the people who wrote I did not know personally. I continued to hear of churches in many places in the world where people were praying for me. I thank you all for your kindness and words of encouragement. May the Lord bless you all.

The local church at Highlands was another place I dreaded to go to. I remember the kind of attention I attracted the first Sabbath I went there! At church, as at the office, Martha and I usually took the front pew. That Sabbath I walked to the front section of the sanctuary all by myself. I sat in our usual place facing the pulpit, all the time aware of all the people behind looking at me. Fortunately, I was not looking at them. The fact that I was a public figure made the ordeal harder to bear. Though I can't say I was as active at the local church as my wife had been, I was nevertheless known by the majority of the church members.

Another public appearance I dreaded was Mandisa and Dominique's wedding. My late wife had been asked by Mandisa to be her matron and the wedding was just a month or so after her death. Mandisa had decided to offer me a special place among her relatives at both the church service and the reception. I believe she wanted to do this to show appreciation for what Martha had done for and been to her. On the Sunday of the wedding, I walked in the company of her father, Dr Chigaru, as everyone watched from the pews. Though I was happy to be honoured by Mandisa,

11. Back at the Office.

I have to admit that it was a very nerve-wracking experience. It made me stand out and obviously made people remember Martha's death. After the service and during the reception, several people approached me to offer their condolences. Though I appreciated their support in that critical hour, I nevertheless felt that that was not the right occasion to offer condolences. I, like everyone else, wanted to be happy and show support to my friends Mandisa and Dominique. Reminders of Martha's death during the happy occasion simply wounded my heart.

The Day My World Caved In.

chapter 12

Advice from 'Experts'.

When death occurs, there are always people who are quick to explain the incomprehensible actions of God as a way, perhaps, to comfort the bereaved. I remember one particular brother who came to my office to offer his condolences. He was the talkative type. He went on as most people had done to express his deep sorrow over the death of my wife. I could tell he was sincere. But maybe in a bid to offer more comfort he digressed into the area of speculation.

'God might have seen that your wife was going to forsake the straight path, so he decided to take her before that could happen,' he offered.

'Well,' I thought to myself, 'why not at least then make the death less painful? Why allow her to die in such a cruel way? And maybe God saw that John the Baptist was going to forsake the straight path; that's why he allowed him to die such a violent death.'

Clearly, this kind of reasoning is unhelpful and out-of-line. It also represents bad theology. God is the only one who knows why Martha had to die the way she did.

A good friend, who hadn't been there when the death occurred, quite correctly encouraged me to take good care of myself 'for the sake of your kids, as they have only one parent now, and that's you.' He implored me to avoid living recklessly in this world of 'incurable diseases'.

Another offered this advice: 'Women will be showing up in a manner you have not known before. Be careful whom you eat with. Some woman with evil intentions may put a love potion in your food so you can love and marry her.'

12. Advice from 'Experts'.

Another elderly friend kept coming to check on me and offered advice on many issues. He had lost a wife himself, and having gone through that experience he knew part of what I was going through. Each time we met, he always remembered to pray for me. My local church pastor Dr Jonathan Musvosvi also checked on me frequently and prayed for me each time he visited. People kept dropping in, either at home or at the office, to see me and to pray for me. It was a wonderful community of believers.

On the issue of remarriage, there were two reigning opinions. There was a side that advised that marrying a single lady who had never been married before would be the best way to go. Their reasoning was that such an arrangement would have few misunderstandings as there would be few third parties. My kids and I would have to deal with her alone and not a situation where there were children and even an ex-husband who was still alive. It would pose a big challenge of communication, they argued. 'If you can't get a single person, the next best solution would be to find a lady who had been married before but had lost her husband and had just one child,' I was advised.

The other group argued that marrying someone who had been previously married and had children was the best way to go. This group reasoned that that arrangement was good in that it would bring balance to our union. Since we both had children, she was more likely to treat my children well than one who had none.

Each case had its own merits, and in the end one needed the guidance of the Lord. God knew what would be best in my situation, and I reasoned that the one who had given me Martha in the first place would surely give me the right person once the issue of remarriage arose.

At that time, it also became common to hear matchmaking stories, especially from women. One woman would mention this name and another one would suggest another. I even heard of a woman who was carrying out a 'search' to find out the woman I was going out with. She was almost at a point, according to the story I heard, of 'concluding the search' and prove which woman I was going out with. As talk like that began to do the rounds, depression was getting the better of me. I just could not understand why people, especially women, relished tale-bearing. One day I talked to a friend about the frustration I was going through because of such stories. She told me not to worry about the stories as 'it is common for everyone in your situation to go through this.'

The Day My World Caved In.

chapter 13

Back to the Birthplace of Our Love.

A month after the death of my wife, I travelled to Chingola, Zambia, to meet with our Adventist believers in preparation for evangelistic meetings we had planned to conduct in September of that year. That meeting was important, because some people had started to think that we were going to cancel the September meetings as result of Martha's death. The local pastor, Kapambwe, organised a meeting of all the churches in the district at Kabundi High School on the Sabbath. Unfortunately, the place proved too small for all the people who came. Just before I stood up to preach, I decided to sing one of the songs I had composed and recorded with Martha and another lady – Chisha. It is a song that talks about the fair land God will give to those who will be saved, a land where there will be no death. As my voice joined the accompanying sound track, I felt a blanket of loneliness cover me as tears welled up in my eyes. A lump stuck in my throat. Sensing the imminent disaster, I quickly closed my eyes, even as I continued to sing.

Martha was once a member of one of the churches there – Chingola Central to be specific. The choir she joined was present that particular Sabbath and many of the choir members had known her. Actually, Chingola was the town where our romance and courtship started. That was way back in 1987. I had brought students from Rusangu Ministerial School for a field school of evangelism. I fell in love with Martha while on that field school trip. Later I was to propose marriage.

I remember vividly one morning when Martha and I took a walk from

13. Back to the Birthplace of Our Love.

Nchanga North Hospital using a lovers' lane known as Consort Avenue. It was a beautiful street that shared a boundary with a well-maintained golf course. I recall stopping at one place along that avenue and telling her that I loved her and wanted to marry her. She never gave me any response. She just stood quietly and looked down. The women of those years were taught etiquette that we don't see in the women of today. In those days, if a man said he loved you, as a lady it was not proper for you to say you loved him too. You had to keep the man guessing for a while before you came out into the open. The idea of not knowing what the woman was thinking added some intrigue and excitement to the whole drama.

I went to bed that night wondering what my baby had up her sleeve. I knew that she liked me, but I could not take matters for granted. The following day I received a letter from her. I can tell you it was a nerve-wracking experience to open that letter. I had to go inside the bedroom of the house where we stayed to find out what the contents were. What she said, however, is a secret I am not willing to disclose.

With hindsight, singing a song on that fateful Sabbath morning that reminded people of my late wife Martha was probably a bad idea. Well, I put up a fight to the end with my eyes closed, but it was clear to many that inside those closed eyes were tears. And, of course, quite a good number in the audience openly shed tears.

In September, when I went back to Chingola for the meetings, I avoided singing and only played our videos over a large screen. People loved them. They actually helped in attracting some of the people to the meetings. Some of the videos we showed were those they had seen on national television. There was a natural desire on the part of some people to come and see George Mwansa in person. Had Martha been alive she would have come with me, for we had planned to celebrate our sixteenth wedding anniversary there where our love was born. We had good meetings which yielded more than three hundred people for baptism into the Adventist Church.

The Day My World Caved In.

chapter 14

St Louis:
meetings, music, friends, sorrow.

Our trip to St Louis, Missouri, USA, had mixed feelings for me. That was going to be one of the great trips we intended to take as a family to the United States. I had planned with Martha that, should funds allow, we would take the children with us for the General Conference meetings to be held that year in St Louis. General Conference meetings are held every five years by the World Adventist Church to conduct business and to elect leaders. We were fortunate that the office was going to fund that trip for us. However, kids were to be taken at our own expense. We felt that taking the kids with us would be a good idea and a wonderful treat for them, especially as we intended to travel to Berrien Springs, Michigan, where we once lived. Our son Brainerd Mwila was actually born there. We felt that they needed to see the place where we stayed and for Mwila to see the hospital at Berrien Centre where he was born. In 2000 during the Toronto General Conference meetings, we had also taken the kids with us and had even travelled to the United States to see our friends May and Mwewa in Waterford near Detroit, Michigan. Afterwards, we visited Pardon and Judy, our friends who at that time were living in Laurel, Maryland. We did not have the time to pass through Berrien Springs. We therefore agreed that we would take the kids there after the St Louis General Conference meetings.

Something, however, had happened. Martha had passed away a couple of months earlier, and I had lost the zeal and excitement to undertake that trip. For the sake of the kids, however, I decided to go. We left Harare

14. St Louis: meetings, music, friends, sorrow.

and made a stopover at Johannesburg International Airport where we met a good number of delegates travelling to the same meetings. In the evening, we started off for Frankfurt, Germany, and arrived early the following morning. The airport in Frankfurt left much to be desired. We searched in vain for a place where we could rest comfortably. I remember hearing my son remark out of frustration: 'This airport is whack!' His sister agreed. I, too, felt it was whack. To compound the situation, our flight to St Louis was scheduled late in the afternoon. We had to move from place to place just to kill time. Another problem was that food was just too expensive. And since we had no visas, we could not even go into the city to look for a hotel where we would have gladly gone to rest before taking the flight to St Louis. There was also no hotel inside the airport. If there was one, they hadn't finished constructing it. It was a very annoying situation. As the long hours dragged their course, I could not help but think of my late wife. If she had been there, her magical touch would have eased the tension. I hated the idea of being asked silly questions by my kids that I sometimes had no answers to. At times I felt sorry for myself, while at other times I felt sorry for my kids for losing such a loving mother. Being a man, I felt so hopeless at handling both the role of a mother and a father.

After what seemed like an eternity at the airport, the jumbo aircraft that was to take us to St Louis took off. However long our journey would take, leaving that airport was a welcome relief.

After the plane had reached cruising altitude and been flying for some time, the cabin crew started serving food, the kind that is often served by airlines (at least in economy class). 'Airline food sucks,' said one frequent flier. My son got a glass of orange juice, and as he fidgeted with something his hand accidentally knocked the glass, spilling its contents on my jacket. Angry, I told him to be aware of his surroundings and sit properly. He could tell that I was not amused, judging by the tone of my voice.

I cannot remember how many hours it took us to fly to St Louis from Frankfurt, but when we arrived it was such a relief. My good friend Pardon Mwansa who had gone ahead of us came to the airport with his son David to pick us up and take us to the hotel. Thank goodness our hotel was just a stone's throw away from the dome where the meetings were to be conducted. That was unlike Toronto, the previous General

The Day My World Caved In.

Conference site, where our hotel was some distance away. I was also impressed with the standards of the hotel. I had requested a room that had two double beds and was quite happy with what I was given. I could tell that the kids were also impressed.

That night as I slept, I could not help but think of my late wife again. My children slept on the bed next to me and I thought to myself how wonderful it would have been if Martha had been around. The kids were going to have a wonderful time. Some of their friends – Paul, Maggie, David, Ernie, Nelly and the Adap kids – were there. Unlike us old fogies who had come for meetings, they had come basically to have fun. Our room became almost a playground for those kids. They would come in and drink canned drinks and eat whatever they could find and just leave cans littered everywhere. One afternoon I came in and found the place in a mess. I tidied up the room, inflamed with feelings of annoyance and wishing Martha was there. In the midst of my righteous indignation, I heard the soft 'voice' of the Holy Spirit: 'Man, have fun with your kids. This is no time to feel stressed. Enjoy the kids while they are there. Time will come when they will no longer be with you.' The tension eased, leading me to smile as I thought about the truthfulness of those words. I resolved thereafter to have a good time with them, whether the room was tidy or not.

During those ten days we were in St Louis, I met many of my friends who had heard about the death of my wife. It was simply another time of sorrow for me. One morning as I was walking with Saustin Mfune to the exhibition hall, I met Mrs Candy Lizardo. Candy is the wife of the former treasurer of the Eastern Africa Division, Jose Lizardo, now working at the General Conference in Silver Spring, Maryland. We worked with them in Harare from 1996 to 2002. Candy loved Martha so much that each time her husband travelled from Silver Spring to Harare, she would give him some stuff for Martha. She always sent very nice things for her. Upon seeing me, Candy just broke down. It wasn't just Candy; I kept stumbling into many such friends who were eager to express their condolences during the whole period we were in St Louis.

St Louis provided a beautiful atmosphere for Pardon's family and mine to take our kids out for eats. At times we took them to Pizza Hut and at other times we went to Ponderosa for buffet meals. The kids loved it.

What I enjoyed most about the meetings was the music. True, I met a

14. St Louis: meetings, music, friends, sorrow.

lot of friends I had not seen in many years. but what thrilled me most was the special music that was presented by groups from all over the world. In fact, for me, this is the number one reason I attend General Conference meetings. I am sorry, my bosses, to make this confession, but to be honest I find the business meetings generally boring. So music is the real stuff for me. I hope that those who have been paying for my past trips won't stop paying after this confession. Obviously I have this bias, being an amateur musician myself. I met groups like The Heralds, and other well-known Adventist singing groups. One female artist, whose name I have forgotten, sang so well that I almost decided to give up singing myself. Her voice in the upper and lower registers was so sweet and powerful that I wondered how some of us could have the temerity to call ourselves singers. The lady is from North America, but married to a Kenyan. A huge guy, with a dreadlock hairstyle, accompanied her brilliantly on the piano.

Then there was a pianist from the Philippines whose rendering of a piece of music was so sublime that I was amazed that a fellow human could perform so well. The huge audience responded with a well-merited round of applause. The standard of music at the General Conference is just terrific.

The Day My World Caved In.

chapter 15

Michigan ...Reminiscing.

After the General Conference meetings were over, my brother-in-law Emmanuel and his wife, Mwila, came to pick us up before leaving for their home in Grand Rapids, Michigan. The quietness and humid summer temperatures of Michigan gave us a rude greeting. Michigan is terrible in both winter and summer. Mwape, who was affected most by the heat, kept the air conditioning running almost all the time she was inside her uncle's apartment. We had a relaxing time at Emmanuel's place. His wife Mwila and their little daughter Bwalya were darlings. While in Grand Rapids we bumped into several Zambian families living there: Silozis, Musondas, Chiyombwes, Kaputos and many others whose names have faded from memory.

The day to visit Berrien Springs finally came. My brother-in-law drove us. We started by visiting the hospital at Berrien Centre where my son, Brainerd Mwila, was born. It used to be called Berrien General Hospital but now has a new name: Lakeland Specialty Hospital. From the hospital, we drove to the house at Berrien Centre where we lived for almost two years. I told my son that he had once fallen from the top floor along the steps leading down to the kitchen as he practised crawling. That was the same house where the little rascal almost drove me crazy with his crying and unnecessary adventurous crawling games.

Once my son learned how to crawl, he liked to create disorder in the house. The week he started to crawl was just unbelievably exciting for him. Within seconds he was able to move to any destination, keeping me

15. Michigan . . . Reminiscing.

wondering where he had obtained the strength. Overnight he was transformed into a heavyweight I could not easily contend with. No matter how hard I tried to perform any tasks, as long as he was awake it was impossible to accomplish anything meaningfully. He quickly established a reputation for crawling to all the wrong places, performing forbidden tasks. He would crawl to the book shelf and remove all the books and scatter them all over the floor. He was fascinated with our hi-fi-system. He would go there, open its glass door and bang it as hard as he could. When I was typing an assignment on my computer, he would crawl under my chair and hit his head against it. He had sharp eyes for little objects. He often picked them up and put them into his mouth. One time he swallowed foil paper.

The boy was also an expert at interfering with other people's work. When I was playing the guitar, he would come and interfere with the strings. When his sister tried difficult tunes on the keyboard, he would stop whatever he was doing and go to interfere with the keys. When we all wanted to sleep, he would bubble with energy and make sure no one got any rest. He would do funny things with his lips and tongue, blowing saliva out of his mouth. He would smile, pull your hair and do all kinds of attention-seeking things so you didn't go to sleep. When he wasn't in a laughing mood, he would make a particular shape with his mouth, appearing as though he had an object there. The boy had so much energy and was disposed to crying so unnecessarily that I made up my mind that I was not going to have any more children.

Evening worship ceased with our boy's arrival in the world. His constant distractions made it practically impossible to have any evening devotions, let alone morning ones. No one wants to lead a Bible study with an angry mind. I tried at first to be a good priest of the home, but the constant unnecessary disruptions from the selfish, silly fellow just made the whole exercise impractical. In the end, the whole thing just died a natural death.

Crying was my son's favourite 'game'. I just don't know why he cried so much. I remember one afternoon, after a particularly exhausting day, he started crying. I was lying on the carpet nursing a back problem created, undoubtedly, by the stress of looking after this ungrateful boy and preparing my perennial class assignments. I just ignored him and let him cry as I had enough of my own never-ending problems. The continued sharp sound of his cry fuelled tension in me. I had resolved, however, not

The Day My World Caved In.

to give in to the little bully, come what may. As the annoying sound grew in intensity, so did the pain in my back muscles. I turned my angry face away from the stubborn bundle, regretting that God had brought him into my life. The noise from the little champion was too much to ignore. I stared back into his face and then into the ceiling so I could blow out my frustration on God. I reminded God that I was also his child and I needed his attention as much as this crazy little boy. 'You will have to take care of this crazy brat,' I said to God. 'After all you are the one who created him.' Meanwhile, the rockstar continued to churn out the raspy, harsh noise, worsening the tension in my back muscles. Rising from where I slept, I grabbed the child and walked to the window where I threatened to throw him out. Oblivious to the danger, the poor child just continued to cry.

Feeding Mwila was always a challenge. The boy had an incredible appetite. No wonder he looked so healthy and bouncy. He ate anything – everything; it didn't matter whether it was African, Indian, European, or Chinese food. And he drank juices, milk and water with the same passion and eagerness. When he was hungry he could not allow delay of any kind, even if that delay was caused by our preparing more food. He did not care about prayer. When he was hungry, he lost all sanity. I remember writing an episode about this phenomenon when he was nine months old:

'These days when my son sees a bowl of food, especially in his hungry state, he becomes impatient and tries to force himself out of my arms, making funny mumbling noises. Once you put the first spoonful in his mouth, it is impossible to turn to any other occupation. The little general will not allow it. Rarely have I seen him leave food unfinished, no matter how much he has eaten. When he is almost full, he likes playing a game that irritates me. He begins to pace about, raising his hands and wanting to touch the food. With sticky fingers he attempts to touch my shirt or any other close object. At times he touches his mouth or his clothes, messing himself up big time.'

The night of 23 December 1993, I had put the little general to bed an hour after his mother left for a night shift. I picked up a book on the life of Florence Nightingale and read it until my eyes began to itch. It was time to go to bed. After I had slept for about an hour, my boy woke up and started to make his usual funny sounds. I gave him his bottle of milk and soon he sucked himself to sleep. An hour or so later, he was up again and started crying. As I was so sleepy and didn't want to be disturbed, I ignored him

15. Michigan . . . Reminiscing .

for a while. He continued crying. I stretched my hand behind his back to stroke him, hoping to send him to sleep quickly. The stroking didn't help as he just continued to cry. I felt my blood pressure rise. 'I won't allow this little brute to bully me,' I said, as anger simmered inside me. 'Why does this rascal have to be so selfish? Each time he wants to sleep, he doesn't want anybody to disturb him, yet when others want to sleep, no matter how exhausted they are, he won't let them.'

The unconcerned boy just kept crying and pushed himself close to my side. In the midst of this fiery ordeal, Mwape, my four-year-old daughter, opened the door to our bedroom and made a beeline to the toilet. When she came out, she stopped and stood by our bedside. 'Go to bed and sleep,' I thundered with indignation. 'There is wee-wee on my bed,' she responded. 'Go and sleep,' I shouted back. She stood defiantly as if challenging me to a brawl. Throwing my blankets aside, I moved out of the bed and took her by the hand to her bed, laying her on the side that was dry, after which I went back to face the misery of my failed sleep as the baby boy continued to cry. 'This is unfair, God,' I spoke in my heart. 'I am tired. Enough is enough. When will this ordeal come to an end? I am angry with you, God.' Finally, I gave the boy his milk bottle which he grabbed like a ferocious lion and emptied all its contents into his mouth. I stroked him on the back and soon he forgot about me as he slipped into dreamland. As for me, I was left wide-awake to wallow in my own misery. There was no one to stroke my back or to give me a bottle of milk.

One winter night in early 1994, I was in the living-room reading a copy of the *Adventist Review* when my daughter Mwape opened the door to the fridge. The night was getting particularly cold and we didn't need any cold air from any source – outside or inside. I smelled my own blood as it began to work its way through the veins at abnormal speed. I had just finished reading a sentence from the magazine that ended with the word, 'spoke.' I shouted at my girl: 'Spoke, speak that door!' My wife laughed as I joined in grudgingly.

Another time while giving my daughter a bath, I turned on hot water from the tap since it was getting extremely cold. (It was actually snowing outside.) As the hot water began to fall upon her young and tender body, she quickly told me that she wanted a cold bath. I knew that she didn't know what she was talking about. And I wasn't in the talking mood. I just proceeded to teach her a practical lesson by turning off the hot water and

The Day My World Caved In.

turning on the cold tap, which was really cold, and let it fall on her. As soon as the cold water splashed upon her body she shouted with excitement: 'I like it. I like it, Dad. I like cold water.' I was dumbfounded.

Mwape did not like the idea of sleeping alone. It was just natural, especially for a girl of four years, seeing that the three of us – Martha, Mwila and I – slept together in one room. I remember writing the following in my diary on 24 January 1994:

'It is after 10pm. Martha and I have to go to bed. Mwila is already in dreamland. We pray and bid goodnight to Mwape. She responds by saying, "Dad, you are my friend also." I say, "Thanks, dear. Goodnight." She responds, "I want to remove my dandruff." (Meaning, "I want to remove your dandruff.") "No, thanks, honey. I have to go to bed now." She looks at me with pleading eyes and insists that she removes the dandruff. Finally I give in and we sleep together. Then her mother comes and says, "Honey, let's go and sleep." The daughter quips: "Dad is my friend." In tit-for-tat fashion, the mother responds, "He is my husband," to which the daughter replies, "No! He is not your husband." We laugh, the mother and I. We continue lying as her fingers scratch my hair. She finally slips away into slumber. Then stealthily and silently I leave the bed and go to join my wife in our bedroom.'

Martha was a great woman. I remembered her long and exhausting shifts at work. She left for work at 6:45am and came back at 3:15pm to another shift at our live-in home for three hours. At the end of those three hours she would come to the upstairs apartment where we lived for another five-hour home shift. That shift was just as gruesome. There was Mwila, our selfish toddler who demanded his own share of mummy's attention. There was Mwape, the calm one, who had her own issues, and not forgetting me, the grown-up baby. Each one of us clamoured for her attention, not forgetting other home chores that ordinarily all men leave for women to do. That she never became insane can be attributed only to God's giving her the strength.

I entered into my wife's world one particular week when, for three days, I slept alone with our son to allow his mummy who had been on exceptionally long shifts to take some deserved rest. By the second night I was looking like a zombie, tired and stretched to the limit by the nine-month-old chubby toddler. On the third night, I was so exhausted that I couldn't hold the fort any more. I made up my mind to take the baby to his

15. Michigan . . . Reminiscing.

mother who was also extremely tired. As I was contemplating doing that, suddenly it dawned upon me that the gruesome task of looking after the baby every night had been my wife's for the past nine months. That realisation strengthened me to stay on with the baby one more night to give my wife an opportunity to sleep without our son's interruptions.

I then saw things from a totally different perspective. For those three days I slept alone with my son, I could not read the Bible for fear that any moment he would wake up and disrupt my good time with the Lord. Suddenly, it dawned upon me how difficult it must have been for my wife to have any meaningful devotional life. When and where would one find the time for prayer? How could one have a meaningful devotional life when one was constantly kept awake in the night by the little bossy general? How could one have a meaningful devotional life when one left very early in the morning for work and continued working until well past midnight? I had made statements in the past to my wife about the need to have a meaningful devotional life. Suddenly I saw how pharisaical I had been. Three days of battling alone in the night with the baby had taught me valuable lessons. If I had been in my wife's shoes, I doubt that I would have even been going to church. I would have been using the hours of the Sabbath to catch up on my sleep. In all those struggles, never did I hear my wife complain about her lot or become sulky in the home. She performed her duties uncomplainingly and was always a good mother to the children and wife to me who only, sadly, took her for granted. Martha was, without doubt, a great woman, mother and wife.

From that house, we drove to the Rosehill Road apartments (then called University Manor) to show the kids where our life in America started. Our apartment had only one bedroom. Martha and I slept in the bedroom while little Mwape slept in the living-room on a couch that was converted into a bed at night. Our son hadn't yet been born.

Our friends Pardon and Judy Mwansa and Goodwell and Rhoda Nthani were also staying at the same apartments. It was at the University Manor that we first had a taste of life in America. We had assumed upon arrival in the great land of abundant opportunities that life would be smooth and sweet. Somehow we had the impression that once we got to Uncle Sam's land of fulfilled dreams, all the loose ends would be tied and life would be one long seamless thread of happiness. Nothing could have been further from the truth. We discovered sooner rather than later that unless one

The Day My World Caved In.

worked very hard, the American Dream would end up just being that – a dream.

We found it strange that there was simply no breathing space in the American fabric of life. We were always on the move. If one was not in class, one was at work. If one was not at work, one was driving to work or engaged in some other such activity. I thought of all the time I had back home when I could visit relatives and friends and just relax. I thought of the long naps I could take without worrying about anything. I wondered why they could call this a land of freedom.

One blistering winter morning, I was driving to work near St Joseph through heavy snow. As I struggled to keep the car on the road, I was suddenly flooded with negative messages: 'What are you doing so early in the morning, driving through impassable and dangerous snow-covered roads in this biting cold?' 'Why did you come to this cold place when you could have been in your home country where it is sunny and warm?' What are you doing in this strange place where work is considered more important than people?' 'Why did you come to this crazy place which is just a hell on earth?' 'Can you honestly say it is sensible to live life in such a crazy way?' In those early weeks I can't remember how many times I was confronted with such negative thoughts. I had never understood why people commit suicide, but now the realisation came. Life wasn't making sense to me. I wondered just how I was going to be rescued from the bondage I had found myself in – the bondage of living in 'free' America.

From the Rosehill Apartments we drove to Andrews University where I was a student in the seminary. I was delighted to see the new and attractive-looking seminary building. Just opposite the seminary is another new building which has also improved the face of the university.

Life at the seminary, generally speaking, was OK. Among others, my friends Cornelius Mulenga Matandiko, who says his other names are Kachiliko, Maikalange, Mfumfumfu, Chinyamantaulwa, Kandanga, now president of the Adventist Church in Zambia, and Stanley Belington Pule Chikwekwe (currently working in Atlanta, Georgia), were my classmates. Other Zambians attending Andrews University then were Brighton Mwanahiba, Tom Ngenda, Goodwell Nthani, Pardon Mwansa, Chola Thewo, Martin Kaoma and Jabulani Munalula.

Attending seminary at Andrews was an unforgettable academic experience. Some of the Adventist theological heavyweights I found

15. Michigan . . . Reminiscing.

included the late Gerhard Hasel, Hans K. LaRondelle and Raoul Dederen. It was a joy to sit at the feet of those men. They were ripe scholars with a wealth of knowledge, and taught with a passion that made them stand out. I always looked forward to attending their lectures.

In all those visits in Berrien Springs, I had a feeling of sadness, arising from the fact that Martha wasn't there to relive the memories with us. It would have been nice to share the sweet memories of the life we had spent together there.

An old cliché has it that whatever goes up must come down. So it was that after two weeks of visiting, it was time to go back. Emmanuel and his wife and their daughter escorted us all the way to O'Hare International Airport in Chicago from where we flew to that 'whack' airport again in Frankfurt, Germany. We spent the whole day languishing at Frankfurt Airport, the same way we had languished on our way to the United States. In the evening we caught a flight to Johannesburg, arriving the following morning and connecting that same day to Harare.

When we arrived home, another important assignment awaited me. My son had been accepted to go to Maxwell Adventist Academy in Nairobi, Kenya, for his eighth grade. He was very excited about that development. He had been praying to attend Maxwell, ever since his sister had started there in 2002. There were also a good number of his friends studying there. David Mwansa, his best friend, had gone there the previous year. In the past this development would never have stressed me, as Martha was there to handle the situation. But now I had not only to prepare for the boy but for the sister as well. Fortunately, Judy Mwansa, Pardon's wife, and Alice Mafanuke, a friend from the office, did a lot to help.

When the day came for the kids to leave for Nairobi, I felt very lonely. I felt lonely firstly because Martha, who was supposed to rejoice with me that Mwila was finally leaving to fulfil his dream of going to study at Maxwell, was not there. Secondly, because these children, the only other people connected to the Mwansa family that came into being on 2 October 1988, were now leaving. I was left virtually alone. It was sad that this empty-nest experience was coming at a time when I had just lost my wife. As I bade farewell to them at the airport to face a dark future alone, I felt abandoned, sad, and dejected. The friends I had gone with, whose kids were also flying to Maxwell, at least had spouses whom they could talk to. I wondered why God had singled me out to suffer this way.

The Day My World Caved In.

chapter 16

Five Years Over; Time For Polls.

During the week of 1-7 November 2005, the St George Hotel in Pretoria became once again a hive of activity for the Adventist Church in the Southern Africa-Indian Ocean Division (SID). Delegates from all the unions, conferences and missions of the division gathered for an important meeting at which leaders of union missions, departmental directors and associate officers of the division were to be elected. Delegates had continued to pour in from every nation comprising the Southern Africa-Indian Ocean Division on the Monday and Tuesday.

The SID, which had been organised in 2002, had barely been on its feet before it was time for elections again. Pardon Mwansa was the first leader of the newly organised entity. Paul Ratsara and Jannie Bekker had been elected secretary and treasurer respectively. Eleven people were elected as departmental directors, and six others to associate officers' positions.

In June 2005, during the General Conference meetings in St Louis, Pardon Mwansa had been elected as one of the general vice-presidents of the General Conference. At the same meetings, Ratsara had been elected as the new president of the Adventist Church in the Southern Africa-Indian Ocean Division to take over from Mwansa. Bekker retained his treasurer's position. Instead of conducting elections for the other elective positions in St Louis, we as SID had decided earlier in the year that we would hold them in November in South Africa.

Naturally, elections are dreaded, especially by those to be subjected to

16. Five Years Over; Time For Polls.

the process. One has to go through them to understand the feeling. Joel Musvosvi, my good friend who teaches at the Adventist International Institute of Advanced Studies (AIIAS), once described the feeling this way: 'As much as you try to be calm as an incumbent, you know that your very being is rocked. As the elections go on, you sit there thinking to yourself, "What will this nominating committee say about my name?" No matter how hard you try to convince yourself that things are OK, there's this eerie feeling, this fear, this anxiety.'

Several factors always come into play during an election of this nature. Whether people care to admit it or not, and whether prayers are offered or not, the element of nationalism from the electorate is always there. Delegates from each country are eager and desirous to see admitted on the SID payroll one or two or more from their country. Thus it is not always a matter of the best candidate getting there. One country could have all the best candidates the organisation might need to fill the slots, but they cannot all be voted in.

Another important factor that plays itself in the election drama is the bias or prejudice of officers towards or against a candidate. The president, in this case, can with wisdom or political skill sway the opinion of the entire committee to vote a name in or out. Generally, the names the president and sometimes his fellow officers want for consideration in the nominating committee will find their place there in one way or the other. At the General Conference, they will normally do a search beforehand of the best candidates who have the potential to fill the vacancy. The president may recommend to the nominating committee a name or names and will often indicate his preference and give his own reasons. In most cases, the president will also allow other names to be cast from the floor for consideration. The nominating committee will then vote names in or out on the basis of detailed and convincing information regarding candidates.

In the division's nominating committee I attended in November 1995 at Mbagathi in Nairobi, there were no names advanced on the floor by the officers. The chairman simply introduced each position, described its functions and the professional qualifications and experience of the individual who was needed to fill it. The floor was then opened for nominations. In every single instance the names of the incumbents were also included. Members and officers alike spoke their minds freely. There

The Day My World Caved In.

was no suppression of any voice by the officers.

I had come to Pretoria seeking God's will for my life. I need to give some background for this statement to make sense. Some time around August 2004 I had decided that I would not seek re-election in 2005. In fact, for a good part of that year I had given much thought to my future, and had come to the conclusion that not only would I not seek re-election, but I would retire from active service in the Adventist Church. I had come to that conclusion after much reflection and prayer. I had taken a careful look at my work as a Communication director for the Adventist Church in the Southern Africa-Indian Ocean Division and didn't see that I was contributing much to the Lord's work in that capacity. My life in the almost ten years I had worked in the Communication department looked dry and empty. At least it did to me. I had a nagging feeling of wanting something better and more challenging, something that would show that I was contributing to the winning of people for Christ.

Time and again I was reminded of the words of a church member who heard me preach at his Chelstone Adventist church in Lusaka, Zambia. That particular Sabbath I had given a mini-musical concert in the afternoon. The following day, a Sunday, I attended a wedding banquet of an acquaintance of mine at the American Dome. While we were waiting for the bride and groom to come, a man I did not know approached me and said he wanted to have a word with me if I did not mind.

'Pastor,' he began, 'I know that you don't know me, but that's fine since you meet many people. I am a member of the church you preached at yesterday. I basically want to tell you that your ministry is not in what you are doing right now. You are a gifted preacher and singer. Unfortunately, these two aspects don't surface much in your ministry. Working in the system has rather closed you out, so that you don't bless the world as much as you would. I don't know why I had to come to tell you this, but I just want to say I have been moved to tell you that you need to consider establishing a ministry that will get you out to the people. In your current job you are being under utilised.'

The words of this stranger cut me to the core. For some time, I had felt that I wasn't really giving the Lord the best of what I could give. I had often told some of my friends that I felt empty just doing the kinds of things I had been doing in communication. The words of that man therefore just confirmed what I had been thinking for a long time. While I

16. Five Years Over; Time For Polls.

didn't think of myself as really being great in both preaching and singing, I did feel, nevertheless, that there was a lot more I could do in both areas than I was doing.

To compound the situation, both 2003 and 2004 were the most depressing years of my stint at the SID. I passed through work-related problems that drowned my morale for work. I concluded, therefore, that in 2005 I would not seek re-election. The question I then had to deal with was what to do next. What was God's next appointment for me? The more Martha and I reflected on these matters, the prospect of retiring became increasingly attractive. If I could retire, I could then do what I have always wanted to do: conduct revivals and evangelistic campaigns. Moreover, I could take my music ministry to a higher level. I could also start writing books and my fascination with owning a radio and television station would become a reality. What an exciting ministry this would be! I thought to myself.

After much prayer and reflection, my wife and I had finally agreed that we would retire from active denominational service in 2005. Having convinced ourselves on the matter we felt that it was time to inform our leader, Dr Pardon Mwansa. One afternoon, I drove to Pardon's place and shared with him what my wife and I had decided. Pardon did not show resistance to the idea, though he was quick to point out important matters we needed to consider as we thought about the implementation of our vision. In the days that followed, Pardon would suggest an idea that either strengthened the vision or deflated it. Generally, however, he seemed to have no misgivings. Our minds were pretty much settled on the idea of retiring, and as days wore on we even started sharing the idea with some of our other close friends.

In December 2004, Pardon and I went for church meetings to Madagascar and Mauritius. In Antananarivo, Madagascar, we attended the year-end meetings of the Adventist Church at the Indian Ocean Union office. (In 2004 the countries that made up that union were Madagascar, Mauritius, Reunion and the Seychelles.) One particular day during a session of the meetings, Pastor Paulo Leitao, the then president of the Adventist Church in the Indian Ocean Mission, brought to the attention of the group the critical shortage of Adventist pastors in the Seychelles. The situation there was so desperate and critical that leadership resorted to placing a call within the SID for a pastor to go and serve there. As I sat

The Day My World Caved In.

listening to the appeal made by Pastor Leitao, I started entertaining the idea of going to the Seychelles in response to that call. That whole day I was consumed with the thought of going there to help, but one thing worried me: How could I bring my own name to the attention of Pastor Leitao without him or others misunderstanding me? True, from the standpoint of benefits and visibility, what I was doing in my present job was by far 'superior'. But God's work is not about fringe benefits and visibility; rather, it is about being where God wants us to be.

For several days, I prayed about the matter. One morning as Pardon and I were relaxing on a beach in Mauritius, I brought the subject up. I told him that I felt impressed to answer the call to serve as a pastor in the Seychelles. 'I am interested to know your thoughts on the matter,' I told him.

'From many fronts,' he answered, 'I consider you to be probably the best candidate. I could personally recommend your name to Pastor Leitao, but your being a personal friend creates a challenge for me.' Although what Pardon said dampened my spirits, it did not throw out completely the urge I had to go and serve as a pastor in the Seychelles. I reasoned that if it was God's will, he would himself find a way for me. After all, it was his work.

In the weeks that followed, the Seychelles dream almost drowned all the other visions I had nurtured. If God wanted my wife and me in the Seychelles because of the need that was there, I reasoned that I could give it a shot for five years and then retire to pursue my bigger dream. The big question was, how could I offer my name for that call? There was at least one good thing even my enemies could not deny. I would not go into this for personal gain. My current position had many attractive benefits that this other job did not have. I reasoned, therefore, that if I found the right person to talk to, he would not read other things into my request. So I decided to talk to Jannie Bekker, our treasurer. I had found Bekker, generally, fair minded in the few times I had seen him on other matters.

I began by sharing with Bekker my intentions to retire, 'so I can do more than I am doing now.' I told him that I had already communicated with our leader Dr Pardon Mwansa. I moved from that subject and told him about the recent trip I had to Madagascar where Pastor Leitao had appealed 'to the division to help us find a person who would be willing to

16. Five Years Over; Time For Polls.

serve as a pastor in the Seychelles.' I told Bekker that after consideration and prayer, I felt that God was calling me to serve there. 'I have discussed it with Pardon, but he feels that being a close friend of mine he is not the right person to handle it. I felt that I could talk to you and hear what you have to say.'

Bekker started by addressing the first issue I had raised. 'Pastor,' he said, looking straight into my eyes, 'when it comes to the subject of retiring, I don't even want you to think about it. God still needs you in the work.' He then went on to give reasons why he felt retiring wasn't a good option at that stage. Moving to the subject of the Seychelles call, Bekker told me how much he had appreciated the ministry my wife and I were engaged in. 'Pastor, I am convinced the few times I have heard you preach at Highlands church that you are a gifted man who can move things. On the other hand, your wife is one of the best pastors' wives I have met. I am convinced beyond a doubt that your ministry to the Seychelles would be a blessing to the church there.' Bekker further encouraged me to travel to the Seychelles to see the situation prevailing on the ground there. He also promised that he would mention my name to the leadership of the Indian Ocean Union when he travelled there in the following days. He emphasised that he would only suggest the name, without putting undue pressure. After prayer we closed the discussion.

Though Bekker never briefed me when he came back, I learned that the church had run into budgetary problems. Accordingly, the matter was shelved. I felt sad as I was prepared to go and work under local conditions because I was convinced that God was calling me there, having laid such a burden on my heart. To me, the issue of salary and other benefits did not matter at all. What was important was simply answering the Lord's call.

Then the unexplainable and unthinkable thing happened. In March 2005 my wife perished in a road traffic accident near Serenje, Zambia. From that time and for the most part of the year, I spent many hours just pondering and praying about my future. The paralysis and trauma of that accident rendered me incapable of thinking straight. I needed to heal. I began thinking of just what God wanted me to do next. Was it his will that I continue with what I had been doing in communication? I have to confess that no matter how much I prayed, nothing seemed to come out clearly from the Lord. I began to think that maybe God wanted me to

The Day My World Caved In.

continue in my work at the SID. However, should that be the case, I trusted that God would confirm it during the November elections.

A week or so before travelling to Pretoria, I met Jannie Bekker and chatted with him briefly about my future. Bekker did not have anything to say specifically, though he prayed for me as he had done many times in the past. He told me to wait for the elections, at which time my situation would become clear. I now have a feeling that even as Bekker spoke with me, he had a very good idea of what was going to happen to me at the meetings. I have come to this conclusion because of what I later witnessed at the meetings. But let's not cross the bridge until we get there.

chapter 17

2005 SID Elections

The SID enlarged committee opened on Wednesday 3 November in the afternoon with newly elected president Paul Ratsara giving a long but interesting keynote address. At the end of that meeting, Pastor Roderick Sithole, executive secretary of the Adventist Church in Zimbabwe, announced that for two days each union and institution represented at the meetings would be allocated time for prayer in the prayer room: 'Every single hour we will have a group in the prayer room for the next two days. Please make sure that you check on the list posted by the door when your turn is to be in the prayer room.' I was impressed with the organisers of those meetings, for that was the first time in a long while I was witnessing such a thing. I reasoned that if we would give ourselves to so much praying, God would, without doubt, be in charge. There would be little room for politics and maybe for the first time God would reveal his will in no unmistakable fashion. We would all be glad with the results of such an election.

That night I went to bed wondering what would be the outcome of the meetings. A lot lay in the manner in which our leaders would let God guide them. Ratsara, who was barely three months in the office, was still in the early stages, where everyone was simply watching to see how he would account for himself as a leader. Some giant test of Ratsara's leadership skills had come. In a few days, we would know what type of a leader he would turn out to be by the way he would handle the meetings.

The following day began with Ratsara taking the morning worship

The Day My World Caved In.

service. His message was appropriate, simple and clear. He shared with us from Scripture what he saw as the method for electing those who were to take up important responsibilities. Before Jesus selected his disciples, Ratsara said, he spent the previous night in prayer. He then went on to tell us that he had no personal agenda in the elections: 'I have given the chairmanship to Jesus Christ and have no agenda in the business of the Lord.' He proceeded to mention that as the nominating committee would be sitting to carry out the business of the Lord, it was his prayer that they would be guided by the Holy Spirit.

I concluded that if Ratsara was going to live by what he said, he would score quite highly and win the hearts of many people. I had personally become tired of leaders who simply used the system for their own political ambitions. They went to the nominating committee to push their agenda and used that committee only as a rubber stamp. I was happy that Ratsara had set the record straight from the outset. I was also happy that the meetings were characterised by prayer. Soon it was time to go into the business of the day. We started the meetings by voting in the members of the nominating committee following a formula tabled by the SID officers. It was simple. Each union was given time to caucus and bring names of people they wanted to serve on the nominating committee. After that exercise, the names of those chosen were brought to the main floor where they were adopted. However, while that process was going on, one member from Botswana raised a point of order: 'Mr Chairman, I have noticed that some unions have included as nominees some people who have served as regular members of the SID for the past three years, while you told some of us not to do that.' Of course, there was nothing in the constitution to suggest that those who had served as regular members for the past three years could not be nominated.

Ratsara quickly stood up to apologise: 'I am very sorry,' he said, 'It was our mistake, but we would like to be consistent. I am, therefore, asking that those unions that elected people like that go back and choose others who have not been regular members.' I saw a handful of people rushing to the microphone to protest. The first to speak was Moses Msimanga, until that time Public Affairs and Religious Liberty (PARL) director at the SID. Msimanga, a pastor and a trained lawyer, was one individual who always spoke his mind freely whenever he felt he had something to say. 'Mr Chairman,' he said, 'would it not be fair if we simply asked those

17. 2005 SID Elections

unions that did not do so to do so, instead of what you are suggesting?' Ratsara stood his ground and insisted that the committee needed to give an opportunity to those who were attending the committee for the first time to be the ones to compose the nominating committee. Clearly, his explanation was not convincing as a queue waited to speak at the microphone. But Ratsara continued to insist that it had to be done that way. Out of respect for the chairman, all those who wanted to say something against his proposal just melted away and sat down. That was a bad omen of things to come. Ratsara scored negatively on that point. There were those who were quick to cite this example after the elections to show that Ratsara had opted to go that way because he wanted to eliminate those who knew the system well, so as not to be challenged in the nominating committee. The final composition of the nominating committee included SID officers, union conference presidents, and General Conference representatives.

The nominating committee was then ready to begin the important and solemn work of electing a new crop of departmental leaders at the SID and new officers of union missions. The rest of us remained in the main auditorium, praying for the nominating committee. After what seemed like eternity, the nominating committee was ready to give the results of the partial report. The nominating committee's task is only to nominate the names. It is the main floor actually that ratifies or rejects those nominations.

The report contained a few surprises. Enock Chifamba, who until that time had been serving as field secretary and stewardship director, was missing from the report. Passmore Hachaalinga, a former president of the Adventist Church in Zambia, who had been working as ministerial secretary of the same entity, was nominated for the second newly created position of vice-president. Gilberto Araujo, the other man in the other vice-president's slot, was widely expected to bounce back. And he did. Among union presidents, Pastor Paulo Leitao of the Indian Ocean Union was dropped in favour of Pastor Samuel Ravonjiarivelo, until then acting president of the Mauritian Conference. Pastor Victor Niconde, president of the Adventist Church in Mozambique, was dropped, and in his place Pastor Zeca Xavier, who had been executive secretary of the same entity, was nominated.

In the second partial report there were no surprises. All the

The Day My World Caved In.

incumbents in associate positions in the secretariat and treasury departments were retained: Julian Hibbert, associate secretary; Jean Mabuto, associate treasurer; Good-son Shumba, associate treasurer and Jacinto Adap, associate treasurer. The third report covering departmental directors at the SID and other officers of union missions could not be given until the following day. The nominating committee met at night to consider the nominations of those particular positions.

It was obviously another night of suspense and anxiety for us whose future was still hanging in the balance. I remember going to bed that night wondering what God's will would be for me. Earlier in the night I had attended a prayer session with fellow directors from the SID: Zacheaus Mathema, Enock Chifamba, Priscilla Ben, Emmiliene Rasamoely, Alexis Llaguno and Moses Msimanga. The mood in the room was sombre. Two days of anxious waiting had taken their toll. We encouraged one another to recall the promises of God as we continued to pray. That night when I went to bed, I kept thinking about my future. Sleep eluded me for a good part of the night. I remembered the words of one friend of mine early that morning as we sat eating our breakfast. He began by asking me a question that puzzled me: 'Do you remember seeing me in the prayer room last night?' Before I could answer, he answered his own question by stating that he had decided that he would not attend the prayers 'because I don't want to be a part of this game they are playing here.' I quizzed him about what he meant. He responded by simply stating that he had sensitive information that he couldn't share with me. I asked him whether he meant that elections would be rigged. 'Just wait and see,' he responded. I told him to his face that rigging would not be possible. I pointed him to all the prayers that we were having and the declaration by the chairman that he had no personal agenda.

'What you are suggesting is not possible. The Holy Spirit is in this place. Let's give credit where it is due,' I said.

'Don't be fooled, George.' His big eyes were popping out as he looked straight at me and paused for effect. 'This whole thing of praying is simply a strategy on their part to hoodwink delegates into believing that the results of the elections are God-guided.'

How could that be? I wondered. If, indeed, that was the plan, it would be tantamount to blasphemy, I reasoned. Blasphemy, because that would be taking the name of the Lord in vain.

17. 2005 SID Elections.

'Just wait and see,' my friend quipped.

I dreaded the prospect of waking up only to be told I had not been re-elected. The cup for me was already full, and something like that could not just complicate matters but worsen them. I did sleep but for only a few hours that night – one of the longest, I must admit.

The morning of Friday 4 November came just like any that had come and gone. I woke up early and joined others for breakfast and later went for the morning devotional. Unknown to me and many in the hall, a decision had already been taken as to whether I would continue at the SID or not. Members of the nominating committee already had that information. All the while I had been pondering on my future and tossing in bed, the members of the nominating committee had known what would become of me. Sitting there in the hall, I remember getting a pat on my back and turning to see Bekker beckoning me to follow him. At that point I knew that the nominating committee had decided that I was not going to be a part of the group that would come back to work at the SID. We had seen that replayed time and again in the hall. Everyone who was called before the officers belonged to the group that had been dropped.

I followed Bekker as he led me to a private room where the other officers and the two representatives from the General Conference were waiting. There was Ratsara, Gerry Karst and my friend Daisy Orion. Karst's face appeared sad, while that of Orion looked sombre. Ratsara's looked rather unconcerned. As he sat down, Bekker just looked down, keeping me guessing as to what was going on in his mind. Judging from past encounters with Bekker, I knew him to be a man who was always helpful and took time to listen each time I went to his office. I could tell Bekker was troubled.

'George, I want to inform you that the nominating committee decided last night not to retain you in your current position,' Ratsara told me in a matter-of-fact way. 'That's fine,' I said. Gerry Karst offered a few words of encouragement and then went on to pray for me. A few minutes later I was out. Well, at least the initial anxiety was over, I comforted myself. I knew that I would not be a part of the new SID team. God alone knew what my next assignment would be.

Crushed by my surroundings and circumstances, I walked back to my room to spend some time with God in prayer. Afterwards I went back to

The Day My World Caved In.

join others in the hall. Later, the nominating committee came to give its final report. From the original eleven departmental directors, only three had been retained. Some, of course, were retired, while others had requested to go on permanent return to their home countries.

To lose one's employment by the ballot conjures up many negative thoughts in the mind. You feel that people have rejected you on account of your poor performance. We all like to succeed and to be congratulated. The vote that dislodges you from the comfort and security zone of your work has a way of playing havoc with your self-esteem. I remember sitting in that hall putting on a brave face, but really wallowing in self-pity. I wondered just what reasons the committee had for voting me out of office. I played repeatedly the negative music of rejection and self-pity and felt a total failure. Fortunately, I remembered that I was not the only one who had been axed.

When you feel rejected by your brethren, the natural thing is to want to isolate yourself. You don't feel like talking to your brethren and the brethren themselves don't feel like talking to you, because they just don't know what to say to you. In the hours that followed that announcement, a surge of loneliness engulfed me. I thought of my late wife Martha, and just wished she had been there, for then I could have found someone to talk to. I felt keen loneliness and wondered why it would please God to batter me from all sides. God knew that I had made up my mind that I didn't want to come back to the SID. He knew how I wanted to go back into pastoral work. He even knew how intense had been my thoughts about retiring. But all those things had been planned in the context of me and my wife working together. God had allowed the one I had been planning to do all these things with to die. After that terrible loss, was it really sensible to be subjected to this kind of treatment? I could not understand why God seemed to be interested in subjecting me to such traumatic experiences. I could not comprehend just what God was trying to achieve.

The following day, my good friend Moses Msimanga met me in the queue during breakfast and joked about the fact that all of us who had been dropped needed to form a support group so that we could start to encourage one another.

chapter 18

Back at the Office in Harare.

Several days later I flew back to Harare to await reassignment. Back at the office several people came to express their sympathy. One of them commenting on the elections said to me: 'Pastor, I could not believe that these officers here could be so heartless. You've just emerged from the terrible loss of your wife, and surely no one could think this could not affect you?' I have to admit that though I explained to this friend that everything works for good to those who love the Lord, I did give some thought to what she said. Death of a spouse has to be experienced in order to be understood. It is one of the most traumatic ordeals anyone can go through. I am not saying that the committee needed to vote me in on account of sympathy because of the loss I had experienced not too long before, but it would have been fair to present my name as well as those of all the incumbents and let the nominating committee decide. After all, that was what had been agreed upon at the office before we left for Pretoria.

At the office, what had happened was dubbed 'Tsunami'. Asked why, someone explained that the office had not seen an exodus of so many people at one election.

That week Bekker called to see me. He asked whether I had received any job offers from anywhere. I told him I hadn't, though informally Cornelius has mentioned that they would like me to go and teach at the newly opened Zambia Adventist University.

'My pastor,' said Bekker, looking straight at me, 'take that offer.' I told

The Day My World Caved In.

him that up to that point I hadn't yet perceived it to be the will of God for me. Bekker promised to pray for me that somehow if it was God's will I would get the impression.

Bekker had a heart to listen every time I presented a problem to him. Generally, problems that were within his ambit to solve, he solved to my satisfaction. Both Bekker and his wife Hanlie took a keen interest in my son. They would often invite him to their house and involve him in musical activities at their church. My son loves the Bekkers very much and always talks about them with great fondness. Bekker and his wife paid a huge bill, arising from my wife's funeral expenses. When I had a problem at the office, Bekker was the one administrator who spoke kindly and understandingly to me.

I didn't know Ratsara that much. We as departmental directors rarely dealt with him. I do remember, though, one incident when he proved helpful. We were preparing to go to the USA for the General Conference meetings in St Louis. I had left the securing of visas for me and my daughter Mwape to the last minute. I had to wait for her to come to Harare as she was studying at Maxwell Academy in Nairobi, Kenya, before we could go to the American Embassy. I remember Ratsara calling me one morning to say that he had made an appointment for me, Mwape and himself, to try to secure visas at the American Embassy. Apparently he had called a person he knew there to assist us. Indeed, when we arrived at the embassy Ratsara introduced me and my daughter to that man. We managed to get the visas. I am grateful for the assistance Ratsara gave us. I also remember the help I got from his wife when I arrived from the funeral of my wife in Zambia. It was Mrs Ratsara who had prepared the evening meal for us that night.

In the days that followed, my time was divided between helping to pack stuff at home and doing one or two things at the office. It was also a time of prayer. I wasn't quite sure what God wanted me to do and where he wanted me to go.

Naturally, when the kids heard that we were going to move away from Harare they were not amused. That was understandable. Of all the places where we had lived, we had spent the longest time in Harare, and it had naturally become their home. After coming back from studies in the USA, we spent about a year in Zambia. The kids were still very young. It was in Harare where both my kids started schooling. Later on they moved to

18. Back at the Office in Harare.

Maxwell Adventist Academy in Nairobi.

Time passed swiftly. Before I knew it, someone from the office informed me that the kids would be coming for the Christmas break in a couple of days. It was, therefore, with a lot of excitement that I went to Harare International Airport to meet them when they arrived. Yes, I was very happy, but strangely sad also that my beloved wife was not there to meet the kids with me. This was Mwila's first holiday and, naturally, I wanted to find out how he had fared, even though we communicated via email almost on a daily basis while he was at Maxwell.

The Day My World Caved In.

chapter 19

Farewell, Highlands Adventist Church Family.

We had been rehearsing briefly for our programme for Sabbath 22 December 2005. It was very important because it was going to be a farewell Sabbath for me and my family. We had been members of the Highlands Adventist church since we arrived in Harare in 1996. Our assignment had come to an end and it was therefore time to go back to our home country, Zambia. I had arranged with each of the people I lived with to participate in the programme in one way or another. At that time those who lived with me were John, Chisha, Besa, Helen, Mwape and Mwila. Justin was also visiting at that time. It was quite a full house. I have always enjoyed a full house. Mwape, Mwila and Chisha were going to participate in music. The rest were to do any of the things that ranged from praying, reading, receiving the offering and leading out in front. I was going be something like a Master of Ceremonies and the preacher.

On the said Sabbath I asked for permission to run the programme as we had planned it at home, and the elder on duty was kind enough to grant us that permission. Chisha sang the special music with Mwila at the piano. Afterwards I took my stand and explained to the church that we were going to have a different programme from the one we normally had on Sabbath.

'I cannot remember how many times I have preached from this lectern in the almost ten years I have been a member of this church. Today I feel that it would be a good idea for others whom I live with also to participate in the programme,' I said to the people. I then went on to

19. Farewell, Highlands Adventist Church Family

introduce the other participants who all sat with me in front. Upon finishing the introduction, I sang a solo, then gave a short, encouraging message from the Bible. Music followed by Mwape and Mwila. I stood up again and encouraged people with another short talk. The programme went on like that for some time until I decided to share some brief thoughts about my late wife's life. I told the congregation that it was sad that one whom we had loved so much wasn't a part of the last programme we were presenting. I went on to talk about how traumatic the sudden and tragic death of Martha had been.

'Without Christ,' I said, 'I don't know how I would have handled this situation.' Jesus indeed had been a dependable Friend – a Friend whom I wanted to walk with all the way.

Upon my ending that talk, Chisha stood up to sing the spiritual, 'I want Jesus to walk with me.' Mwape was at the piano to accompany her. Chisha managed to sing one verse, but when she moved to the verse that says, 'In my sorrows, Lord, walk with me,' she began to break down. She tried to drag herself on but the damage was done. She stood there and just broke into sobs. I then stood up to hold her and somehow comfort her, but suddenly I felt a current of emotion sweep over me like a flood. Holding her with my right hand, I stood there with tears flowing in front of more than three hundred people. Justin who was seated with us in front helped us to sit down. By that time everyone in our group was crying. Mwape who had been playing the piano just left her seat and went to cry outside. John who was busy taking the video could not stomach what he was witnessing. He was overcome like all of us and just stopped shooting. Tears started to flow down his cheeks. Helen and Besa who sat next to us were also in tears. I continued to wipe my tear-stained face. I have no doubt that a number of people in the audience were also sobbing. The only ones in our party who did not cry were Mwila and Justin. Justin, himself a minister of the Gospel, stood up and gave an impromptu sermonette, punctuated with singing.

That was indeed strange, because at the time we were rehearsing there was nothing to indicate that it would all end that way. Had we known that something like that was possible, we could have avoided the use of the song that brought all of us to tears. In all my life I had never imagined that I could cry in front of the church, but it happened. What a way to say goodbye to the people!

The Day My World Caved In.

In the evening there was to be a farewell party, organised by the church, for us in the church hall. That was one party I wasn't comfortable to attend because I thought that only a few people would show up. But I was proved wrong. It was one of the best-attended farewell parties I have ever known at Highlands church. We had a very good time. There were speeches and plenty of music. A couple by the name of Mr and Mrs Dimairo shocked everyone by performing. One has to know Mr Dimairo to appreciate this. He is by nature a quiet fellow. His wife is the exact opposite. Mr Dimairo talks only when it is really necessary. When it was announced that Mr and Mrs Dimairo were going to give us a song, I thought it was just a joke. I didn't think Mr Dimairo would be the kind of person who could sing a special song in front of people. But I saw him rise not only to his feet but to the occasion. The couple sang in the funniest way one could imagine. At one point in the singing Mr Dimairo even started to add actions to his singing. It was so funny that I almost died laughing! Before we ended the programme I went to the Master of Ceremonies and asked for permission to say something.

'When I was coming here this evening,' I said, 'I didn't think I would find so many people. This is one of the best-attended farewell programmes I have ever known at this church. I didn't realise that people loved us so much.' The statement made some people laugh.

A few days later it was time to think about Christmas. I do not enjoy Christmas. But Mwape while at school had written to suggest that we should plan to make Christmas special. In view of Martha's death, I decided to give the kids a memorable time. They invited some of their friends, and a few of my friends joined us. The partying dragged on late into the night. Of course, the absence of Martha had a dampening effect on my soul, in spite of the Shona saying that goes: '*Asipo hapo.*' (The one who is not there, is not there. Just go ahead and enjoy the fun.)

Early in the month of December (6 December to be specific) the SID office organised a farewell party at a Lebanese restaurant in Harare for the outgoing departmental directors. Ratsara gave a short speech in which he stated the reasons for having such a party: 'We are here because of the nature of the Adventist work. As you all know, this is the Advent Movement. For some of our friends the time has come to move on to other responsibilities while others are coming in.' He then thanked those of us who were leaving and promised to remember us in prayer.

19. Farewell, Highlands Adventist Church Family.

The function closed after a brief presentation of gifts. The last meal had been served, signifying the end of my stint at the Southern Africa-Indian Ocean Division. My mind had to shift to an unknown future. Life at home had taken some new lease of energy with the coming of Justin from Cape Town, where he had just completed his theological studies at Helderberg late in November. Justin is an interesting character with whom I share many things in common. My kids love him and he has a very good rapport with them. I was happy that he had come to visit.

One morning in mid-December I unexpectedly received a phone call from Mrs Christine Tembo, a receptionist at the Seventh-day Adventist Church headquarters in Lusaka, asking me to send my CV, ministerial credentials, transcripts and copies of my academic certificates by fax. 'If it is possible,' she said, 'send them today, as the Zambia Adventist University board will be meeting soon.' Mrs Tembo had been asked to phone me by Dr Cornelius Matandiko, president of the Adventist Church in Zambia. Matandiko had been attending meetings in Livingstone at the time the phone call came.

Though it was not an official call, I understood, at least, that what Matandiko had earlier discussed with me was what he had chosen to take to the committee. I went to the office that afternoon and thought seriously about the matter. After several weeks of praying and contemplation, I still did not have any strong impression that that was where the Lord wanted me to go. I found it to be rather strange, especially in view of the fact that I enjoy teaching. In the evening I asked several people to join me in prayer that God might somehow guide me into making a decision.

Several days later while I was still in this wilderness of indecision I received a phone call from Solusi University, asking whether I would be interested in joining the faculty of Theology and Religious Studies. I considered it for a few days then decided to accept the call. The prospect was attractive, so I was inclined to give it a try.

In January 2006 I moved to Lusaka, Zambia, where I stayed as I waited to take up the service call to Solusi University in Bulawayo, Zimbabwe, in May.

The Day My World Caved In.

chapter 20

First Anniversary of Martha's Death.

The month of March arrived like others before it in the New Year, 2006. In the next several days it would be one year since my dear wife Martha passed away. As the days drew closer to 6 March, I began wondering just how the day would be. A couple of days before the fateful day of commemoration, I received some text messages from a friend who had lost a husband years earlier on 8 March.

She wrote: '8 March used to be my grieving day. God healed me over time. He will do the same for you.' She followed it up with another that said: 'Some promises to think about: Isaiah 26:19 and Revelation 21:1-5.' As if that were not enough, that good friend again wrote: 'To me, 6 March marks the end of a very critical year when God was literally holding you together. I no longer fear for you.'

As the day drew closer, another friend wrote to me, assuring me that many friends were praying for me. As for me, I began thinking seriously of how I was going to commemorate the day. I reasoned that going to the graveyard where she lay awaiting the Second Coming of our Lord and Saviour Jesus would only bring grief and despondency to my heart. The Lord in his wisdom had allowed that wonderful lady to rest. I had to think of something positive I could do on that day. I reasoned that being the wonderful person she had been to people she could be remembered by my buying food for street kids and a few people at the hospital. When 6 March came, I spent most of the day by myself. thinking about the wonderful time God had allowed me to spend with Martha. With the help

20. First Anniversary of Martha's Death.

of my brother-in-law John, I distributed food as I had planned.

In the evening I visited my sister-in-law, who, with my brother, had survived the accident. I went with Justin, who was visiting me from Ndola. I found my sister-in-law at home. We asked the children who were around to be present as I briefly shared what I went through that Sunday of 6 March 2005, when Alex and Martha died. I went on to encourage everyone around to think seriously about the brevity of life and how important it was to have our lives always anchored in God. My sister-in-law could not contain herself. She began to sob as we all watched her in sympathy. Afterwards, I asked Justin to pray, after which we left.

The Day My World Caved In.

chapter 21

Remarriage, My Kids' Views.

A week or so after the commemoration of Martha's death, my kids arrived from Maxwell Academy in Nairobi. I drove to the airport to pick them up. We drove to my new apartment at the office compound in Lusaka. I could tell that the kids were not impressed. Not that there was something particularly wrong with the apartment, but I guess lack of the many things they had been accustomed to play with at our Harare home contributed towards the general despondency. Our goods had not yet come from Harare. I was very happy to see them, though they didn't fancy the idea of staying with me at my apartment. They wanted to go to the Chibendes' where there was plenty of fun since their friends from school were there. Mwape asked if she could stay at her friend's house. Tina Matandiko lived just a stone's throw from the Chibendes'. While I didn't object completely to their moving out, I felt sad that my own kids who could help bring some bright moments into my life were already thinking of leaving me. The thought of their leaving just intensified my loneliness over the loss of my dear wife Martha. Not wanting to stand in their way, I allowed them to go and stay at their friends' homes for a few days. I reminded them that I had been missing them and also wanted to be with them.

One evening after they had come back from their visit to their friends, I asked them to accompany me to the University of Zambia where I was conducting revival meetings. I wanted them to join the musicians who were performing that evening. They graciously accompanied me and even

21. Remarriage, My Kids' Views.

participated in the programme. I was happy that they had both become competent enough to play instruments in front of a big audience.

A few days later I called them to one of the rooms in the apartment and told them that I wanted to discuss something important with them.

'Guys,' I said, 'I want you to be brutal in your honesty with me over what I shall ask you. You are my kids, needless to say, and I need to know your thoughts on the matter I am about to introduce.' They both looked at me attentively and just wondered what it was I wanted to discuss with them.

'You are aware that it's been now a year since your mum passed away.' I paused as I searched for the best way I could express what I was about to say. 'Life has not been easy for us all and it is only by the grace of God that we have survived this far,' I said. 'Through these many months there are things I have felt I have not done well because of being a man. I think especially of the difficult times I go through when you guys are about to leave for school. Your mum knew exactly what needed to be done, where to get what and so on and so forth. I feel from that angle that I need someone who could be there to help me look after you guys, a woman who would be your mother. But not only from that angle. There are times I feel lonely and want to be with someone. You guys often want to be with your friends and I just have no one to be with. Now I've called you here so that you can give me some thoughts on the matter I have raised. I want you – let me repeat – I want you to be brutal in your honesty. Tell me exactly what you feel about this matter.'

Mwape, the lady of the house and the older one, was the first to speak. 'I understand what you are saying, Dad.' She looked at me with a smile on her face, revealing dimples. 'I can tell you are lonely. Personally, I don't mind your getting another wife. The only thing that bothers me is when I think about what kind of a mother she will be. Will she be treating us nicely? Honestly, that's the only thing I often worry about.'

Her brother Mwila, itching to pick the topic up, gave his point of view: 'You know, Dad, the other day when we accompanied you to the university I could tell that you were lonely. I saw you standing alone and I just said in my heart, "This guy is lonely." ' I could not help but burst out laughing. He continued: 'But, as Mwape has said, the question that bothers me most is whether that mother will be nice to us. I know, Dad, you need to marry some day, but I just wonder how that mother will be to

The Day My World Caved In.

us.'

'In the old days,' I said, 'things were different. If in the family of your late mother there was someone they could give to me and I liked her, she could become your new mother.' I went on to give the example of their aunt Mary, my late wife's young sister. 'That's weird,' Mwila countered. 'I can't think of Auntie Mary becoming our new mother when all along she has been our auntie.' His sister agreed: 'Yeah, it just won't be easy for us suddenly to start calling her Mum. I think another woman is better.'

'Guys, we are in this thing together,' I said. 'We must pray that God will help us to find the right wife for me and the right mother for you.'

At another time my son and I were going through pictures on my laptop. I can't remember what precipitated the discussion on my getting a new wife. I asked my son how he would feel calling my wife his mother. 'Of course it will sound weird.' I laughed and asked him why. 'Dad, even you,' he responded, 'would feel the same if your dad married another woman.'

'In that case,' I countered, 'what would help is for you to get to know the woman before she gets in the house.'

'That's true, but we shall start by calling her Auntie, and when she comes into the house we shall call her Mum. That's kind of weird.' I broke into one of those laughs where every muscle cries out in pain.

On another day my children and I were having a chat when I brought up the subject of marriage. 'Guys,' I began, 'what do you think of the idea of having a few more children if I remarry?' I told them that their new mother would most likely want to have one or two children. I was surprised that both didn't seem to mind. They didn't have much to say, but the little they said suggested that it was an idea they would be comfortable with. A couple of days after that discussion, Mwape brought up the subject again. I found her working in the kitchen when she said, 'Oh yeah, Dad, you remember that discussion about your having more children? Last night I was thinking about it and thought it would be a good idea so that I could also help you take care of them.'

'Cool,' I said. Mwape is sweetly disposed towards little ones. In fact, this is one thing my kids seem to share. They both have tender feelings for little ones.

One particular night at my brother's place in Lusaka when Mwape and I had been visiting, I went to bed feeling ill. I had a fever and a headache

21. Remarriage, My Kids' Views.

with general physical pains. As I lay in my bed I called Mwape to bring me water so I could take some painkillers. When she entered she found me in blankets. I was feeling quite bad and the temperature was rising. I groaned with pain as my helpless baby watched. Smiling in a rather naughty way, she remarked: 'Dad, I think what you need is a woman.' I smiled back and told her that wasn't true. She then went on even to suggest the name of a woman and I just gave her a mute response.

One night at Solusi University, I came back from teaching exhausted, and found Mwape in the kitchen engaged in some work. The poor girl had been struggling that whole day trying to cook beans. She had never cooked beans before. I couldn't help much as I could not remember cooking beans before. Earlier in the day she had switched off the stove after she thought the beans were cooked. When I tasted them, I discovered that they weren't really cooked as they weren't soft. I asked her to add water and give them longer to cook. While she was in her bedroom resting, the water in the beans dried up, causing the bottom of the pot to get burned. That evening when I returned from work she was feeling rather tired and frustrated. I met her in the kitchen and told her how sorry I was that she had to go through that ordeal.

'My baby, I am sorry about this. I feel bad that you have to think about what to cook, especially when our food is in such short supply. I also feel bad that you have to act like the mother of the home at such a tender age.'

Solusi was a long way from Bulawayo and often even simple things like vegetables had to be purchased in town about 53km away.

'Dad,' Mwape said, her face showing her frustration, 'you need to marry because I can't manage to do what I am expected to do. We must have the right person to take care of home matters.'

105.

The Day My World Caved In.

chapter 22

The Wilderness Experience.

I moved to Solusi University in May 2006. John came along and stayed with me for a few weeks. Later, Mwape, Mwila and Besa also joined me. After a while, however, all of them left. Mwila left for Maxwell Academy in Nairobi while Mwape went to live with her uncle Emmanuel in Grand Rapids, USA, to conclude her high school education. Besa left for the Philippines to study nursing while John went back to Zambia. As far as I can remember, that was the first time in all my life that I was going to live alone. After completing high school, I went for national service and later joined the Adventist Church, working as a translator. The one year I served as a translator, I lived with other single guys, James Chapi, (now a pastor in the North Zambia Field), Kalaba Kapambwe (presently district pastor in Chingola, Zambia) and Pardon Mwansa (currently serving as vice-president of the General Conference). Later, Pardon and I went to Solusi to study theology.

When I completed my BA in theology at Solusi University, I was posted to Kalulushi, a small mining district in Zambia, where my friend Pastor Kalaba Kapambwe and I served together. We actually lived in the same house as we were both still single. It was such a joy working with him. Though he can sometimes be hard, he has a sweet and congenial personality. He likes making rib-cracking jokes and I really like him very much. I thank God for giving me an opportunity to work and live with Kalaba Kapambwe. Later on when I moved to Monze town in the southern province, to teach at Rusangu Ministerial School, I lived with

22. The **Wilderness** Experience .

Justin. Justin, who is now a big guy, is married and serves as a pastor in Ndola.

Then, suddenly, life was dragging me into something I had never been prepared for. And to make matters worse, the economic situation in Zimbabwe had changed so drastically that life became unbelievably hard. Our university, located 53 km outside Bulawayo, Zimbabwe's second largest city, had become a wilderness in every sense of that word. In the days I had studied there, we had a thriving, mechanised farm where they produced all kinds of things. We had a scientific garden that was in a class of its own. They grew a variety of vegetables that looked so healthy one wondered how they did it. The local shop was stocked with virtually everything one could think of. At the cafeteria, they generally cooked standard mouth-watering meals. In those days, we had people coming from Bulawayo to buy goods from Solusi. Then Solusi had changed completely. True, it had become big in terms of infrastructure development and student enrolment. At the time I was there as a student we were fewer than 300. Then, the number had risen to more than 2,000. There were a few imposing building: the Ralph Watts Library, the men's Raelly Hall, the ladies' Sweden Hall, the assembly Beit Hall, and a few more plant infrastructures. But while things looked imposing from the outside, the new Solusi was not as comfortable to live in as the old and small Solusi of yesteryear.

At Solusi, communicating with the rest of the world proved daunting. While the campus' population warranted a mobile phone network, none of the three phone companies provided that facility. It's true that in certain points at the campus, one could stumble into a Net One, Telecel, or Econet network, but Solusi wasn't yet connected. Actually, Net One had already put up a tower and there had been talk that Solusi would soon be connected, but it remained just that – talk. Phoning from the reception using the land-line wasn't easy either. To compound the situation, there was no proper Internet connection at Solusi. Except for a brief period when the computers in the faculty lounge worked, each time I wanted to communicate with my loved ones, I had to travel to Bulawayo.

Cooking posed the biggest challenge to my new life. While I know how good food tastes, I have to admit that when it comes to how good food is cooked, I am a freshman. Not only am I a freshman, but I am uninterested

The Day My World Caved In.

in preparing meals. Some people say I am lazy when it comes to cooking. If lack of interest is synonymous with laziness, then I am lazy. If this be the case, I can only hope that I it will be a vice I can manage to overcome.

I would drag my feet to the kitchen and just stand as I took stock of the items that were staring me in the face, the most conspicuous ones being the fridge and the stove. The million-dollar question would then pop up: 'What shall I cook?' I would stare at the scanty food items and often just walk out of the kitchen in frustration. The kitchen was a torture chamber for me.

One morning, I set myself the challenge of cooking beans. Those of you who know how beans are cooked know that it takes the whole day to cook them. I started by soaking the beans and then put them in a pot and filled it with water close to the brim. Every so often I would check the water level and pour in more. In the afternoon, a friend of mine came to pick me up for some meetings I was conducting in Bulawayo. Unfortunately, I forgot to switch off the stove. While in Bulawayo I remembered that I had left a pot of beans cooking on the stove! I prayed that God would perform the miracle of a power cut at Solusi University. I reasoned that I wasn't asking too much from God, knowing that shed loading was a daily feature not only at Solusi but the entire country of Zimbabwe. Undoubtedly as I was praying for God to perform that miracle there were other people on the campus of Solusi praying that there would be no power cut that night. Naturally I was anxious to know whose prayer God would answer. I reasoned that since I had gone to Bulawayo to preach the Word of God, God would be more interested in answering my prayer than those of others praying that there should be no power cut. Five hours later when I got back to Solusi my house was covered in smoke. The beans in the pot were reduced to ashes. The pot itself had lost some of its iron elements. It took more than three weeks for the smell of smoke to clear completely from the house.

One evening I arrived from town after a particularly eventful day. Tired and hungry, I longed to get home and force myself to prepare something to eat. As we were approaching the gate to the campus, I noticed that the whole place was in darkness. Reaching the house, I opened the door and fumbled through the darkness to search for a candle and a matchbox. Before I could locate the two items, it dawned on me that I could not use the candle to cook whatever food there was to be cooked. 'Why waste

22. The **Wilderness** Experience .

my time looking for something that won't help me cook the food?' I reasoned with frustration. Angry with the leaders in Zimbabwe, God and myself, I retired to the bedroom and threw my tired frame onto the bed. Looking into the dark and formless nothingness, I brooded over my fate. I remembered the words of my son: 'Dad, I don't understand why things just don't seem to go well for us ever since Mum died.'

Travelling to town also became a nightmare. The fuel situation had become so bad that it was next to impossible to find fuel at petrol stations. In a few selected stations where fuel was found, you had to have coupons in order to buy it. As a rule, only those with foreign currency got their fuel using coupons. The rest – who were the majority – got it only God knows how. At times even when one had coupons, fuel was not available. In some cases when it was available, one had to queue for it in a long column of vehicles. One afternoon, I happened to find myself in one of those long queues. I waited patiently at the tail end of the queue for my turn to come as we moved at a snail's pace. As night began to cover the Earth, I drew close to the pump and was glad that at long last I would soon be getting my share. However, just when I was about eight vehicles from the pump, power suddenly failed. The petrol attendant said in a matter-of-fact way, 'Come tomorrow.'

I left that place angry again with the Zimbabwean authorities for letting the fuel situation linger so long without finding a lasting solution. My mind was taken back to the year 1999 – late that year – when the fuel crisis started. I couldn't understand why those in responsible positions had not found a solution to such a critical and strategic area of the national economy. That evening, I remember complaining to a friend about the never-ending problems I was going through. I found it rather frustrating going through such harsh realities when I could simply go back home and live a normal life. I told my friend that I would not mind enduring the difficult life in Zimbabwe if I knew that my work was bearing fruit. 'Why should I suffer like this?' I asked. It was clear that I had reached breaking point. I thought of the advantages of going back home and serving God in evangelism. 'Don't you think,' my friend quipped, 'that you are actually doing more for God at Solusi University training ministers than serving as a pastor in some city in Zambia? And one good thing in your job is that you have students from all over Southern Africa.' Maybe my friend was right, but I was just too exhausted

The Day My World Caved In.

that night to think objectively.

Comments from a few students about my being distant and closed concerned me deeply. 'You are always just alone. Why don't you have friends here?' they would ask. Apparently, students were not the only ones who held the view of my being distant. One Sabbath morning as I was coming out of church, Ms Mhosva, a member of faculty who had also lost a partner through a tragic road accident, confronted me about being distant.

I tried hard to find reasons for this state of affairs. I reasoned first that that had more to do with the fact that generally I am not an outgoing type of character. My phlegmatic temperament is not that of an extrovert.

I am not like my friend, Saustin Sampson Kagzeba Mfune, who has a sanguine temperament. Saustin enjoys talking. Laughing and cracking jokes is his way of life. Saustin bubbles with energy and can talk from morning to evening. I don't know where he gets the strength from. I talk only when it is necessary.

Another thing: Solusi, generally speaking, is a busy place. It's not easy to find time to socialise. Life in an academic setting has its own rules. Even my good friend Enoch Chifamba, who is a very friendly person, rarely checked on me. His wife had to remind him time and again to 'check on your friend George and see how he is doing.'

Let me also add that losing a spouse is devastating. It's often hard for one to muster the strength to do anything. One needs a lot of support from friends. Writing from the perspective of one who has experienced the loss of a spouse, I advise the community of faith to embrace those who are grieving, especially ones like myself who are living alone. Coupled with this reality was the fact that my children were gone. I missed them terribly. I am sure that affected me in ways I might not even have anticipated.

However, despite the things I have said on this issue, I feel bad to this day that I was viewed by some students as being unfriendly. I don't know how many times I have prayed that God would help me to be like him, to have a face that does not offend and put off people. The kind of work I do requires the cultivation of social graces that help one to make a correct representation of God. I desire to be friendly. I am sorry that I have made very slow progress in this area. In the morning when I wake up it's always my prayer to God that he will give me a sweet disposition

22. The **Wilderness** Experience.

and a happy face. I always pray that in my quietness I shall wear an attractive countenance that will draw people to Christ.

To run away from the insanity of living alone and cooking, I usually left campus on Thursday afternoon for Bulawayo and came back only on Monday morning. I spent my weekends at my friends Evans and Silvia Muvuti's house. Muvuti at the time of writing this segment of my story (November 2007) serves as president of the Adventist Church in Zimbabwe. Muvuti's wife, Silvia, and children Tinotenda, Faith and Delight looked after me exceptionally well. They never got tired of hosting me every time I went to their house.

I first met Evans when I went to study theology at Solusi University in the early 80s. He was then just a single guy like me. The thing I remember well about my relationship with Evans, during our stint at Solusi, was the noise we used to make in a cooking class taught by Mrs Siwardi, widow of Naison Siwardi who had been business manager of Solusi College. Evans was a good guy who enjoyed a good laugh. Later we stumbled into each other again at Helderberg College in South Africa, where we took classes together for a Master of Religion degree offered by Andrews University.

Later, when I moved to Harare to serve as Communication director for the Eastern Africa Division, Muvuti was our pastor at the Highlands Adventist church I attended. His wife Silvia and my late wife became very good friends. As families we often visited each other. After serving for a couple of years as pastor of Highlands church, Muvuti moved to the East Zimbabwe Conference where he became the executive secretary before becoming president of the same entity. Not long afterwards he moved to the Adventist Church headquarters in Bulawayo to become the executive secretary. When Solomon Maphosa who served as president of the Adventist Church in Zimbabwe left, Muvuti became the president of the big church entity.

God used the Muvutis to minister to my social needs. I shudder to think how my life would have been without their presence in Bulawayo. I thank Silvia and Delight, the two people who were always around to take care of my various needs. I shall be eternally thankful to the Muvutis for the kindness and hospitality they showed me in my time of bereavement.

One evening, I remember feeling particularly low. In the midst of all my unending blues, I wondered what I was doing at Solusi. I felt as though

The Day My World Caved In.

my work there was simply an unnecessary detour. That evening, I walked to the office to check on something. I found our dean's secretary, Gertrude, working. I stopped by for a brief chat. While we were talking, I saw on the dean's table a large envelope bearing my name. I picked it up and opened it. Inside were evaluation papers from my students in the three courses I had taught the previous semester. Naturally, I was anxious to see their comments. What I read convinced me that my trip to Solusi, after all, had not been in vain. In all the three courses I had taught, the students were so generous with their comments that I felt the cloud lifting. I was convinced God had brought me to Solusi. Later I was to scoop the award of best Solusi University male lecturer for the second year running.

One afternoon, I was driving from Victoria Falls town to Bulawayo. I had paid a short visit to Lusaka, Zambia, and was then going back to Solusi. About 15km before Lupane, a small town between Hwange and Bulawayo, I stopped to rest as I was feeling rather drowsy. As I stood outside the car trying to chase away sleep, I heard a popping sound from the engine. Not being a mechanic, I dismissed it and didn't even care to open the bonnet to find out what had caused the sound. Fifteen minutes later I started off. After driving for about 2km, I felt the vehicle losing power, despite the pressure I was exerting on the accelerator. I checked my temperature gauge and much to my horror it had shot up to the very end of the red zone. I smelt trouble and immediately pulled the vehicle to the side and stopped. I opened the bonnet to be met by smoke from the engine. In several places I even saw fire which I managed to extinguish. With the eyes of a layman I checked the engine to detect what was wrong but discovered nothing.

I phoned Tom, the mechanic who normally worked on the vehicle, and explained what had happened. Of course there was nothing Tom could do as he lived in Harare, more than five hundred kilometres from where I was stuck. He asked me to call somebody to tow me. I called a friend who immediately started looking for help and promised to call later. While I was waiting – obviously in despair – a Good Samaritan, whom I had earlier overtaken, recognised my vehicle and stopped. He asked what was wrong and I gave him details of what had happened, though I didn't know what and where the problem was. His knowledge about vehicles seemed to be average, and therefore way above mine. After checking a

22. The **Wilderness** Experience.

few things on the engine, he identified what had caused the problem. The rubber pipe that carried water from the radiator to the other parts in the engine had come off. All the water in the radiator had therefore been drained, affecting the entire cooling system. Those who have a knowledge of vehicles will know that that was a very serious problem. The only thing we could do was tow the vehicle to Bulawayo, a distance of almost 200km from where I was. Unfortunately, we didn't have a tow bar. The good man left afterwards and wished me God's speedy help.

My friend from Bulawayo later phoned and told me that she had arranged with the driver at the Zimbabwe Union Conference, a Mr Moyo, to come and tow me. However, since it was getting late, Mr Moyo could only come the following day. I kept hoping that another Good Samaritan with a tow bar would stop by and help me but that did not happen. The message from the sun was not encouraging either. Soon, the big ball disappeared from the sky and only God knew what was to become of me. For some time I just stood outside the vehicle, thinking about how God had been shaping my life. Frankly, I wasn't amused. I just couldn't figure out what God was trying to do with me. It seemed to me that God had suddenly taken a strange delight in causing me every imaginable form of pain. Theology was quick to remind me that it was not God bringing those problems but Satan. True, but God was allowing him, I countered. And ultimately, I held him responsible for my pain. I reasoned that God had the power to prevent that rubber pipe from getting off its place. My sore throat couldn't help matters. Trying to drink water and indeed even swallowing saliva was a struggle.

When it became dark I got into the vehicle, reclined the front passenger seat and slept. Minutes later my mobile phone rang. Another friend from Bulawayo was on the line to share his sympathy. 'It's dark out here,' I said, 'and there is no village nearby. I am sure I shall spend the night with animals. I am not afraid though. I have opened the front windows just high enough to let in some fresh air.'

'Some time in the night when you wake up and look through the window,' my friend quipped, 'you may just see this big lion looking at you trying to figure out how to get its meal.' We laughed. I was reminded of the story my friend Enwell Kadango told me while on a visit to Malawi. According to Enwell's story, a lorry with passengers at the back was on its way to Mzuzu in northern Malawi. After a slow ascent through a

The Day My World Caved In.

mountainous terrain, the lorry was about to begin its descent when a hungry lion waiting by the roadside jumped in the back of the lorry. The lion's intention was to catch and kill one of the passengers for its meal that day. Unfortunately for the lion (and fortunately for the people), the forward movement of the vehicle caused it to jerk forward, backwards and sideways, causing it to lose stability. Instead of concentrating on its original intention of making a kill, it then faced the challenge of maintaining its balance in the moving lorry. According to the story, which Kadango said was true, when the lorry arrived in Mzuzu the lion was shot while the vehicle was still moving.

As I lay on the seat, my thoughts about the lion dissolved and shifted to my Toyota Emina mini-bus parked at a friend's garage in Lusaka, Zambia. I had bought that Toyota from Japan in 2004. One day while driving it in Lusaka, the vehicle just stopped suddenly. I couldn't figure out what was wrong. I called a mechanic who towed the vehicle to his garage. He quickly diagnosed the problem. The timing belt had snapped again. That was just two weeks after we had replaced the old one which had snapped and caused a lot of damage to the cylinder head and other key parts. We had spent time looking for the parts everywhere around Lusaka, and when we found them they were very expensive. I could not understand how a new belt could snap just like that. The story of my Toyota Emina is a long and frustrating one. Let me just cut it short by saying, the belt was 'chewed' four more times before I finally decided to throw in the towel. Strangely, my able mechanic also couldn't figure out what was causing the snapping of the belt each time a new one was put on. And every time the timing belt snapped it destroyed on the engine key parts that had to be replaced at astronomical expense. I have never spent so much money on any vehicle as I spent on that car. It literally wiped out my bank account. Each time the belt snapped, I kept wondering what lesson God was trying to teach me. Frankly, I failed to discern the moral.

Now barely after just a few months of my driving this Mitsubishi Pajero I had bought from a friend the unthinkable had happened. What crimes had I committed against God to have such a string of misfortunes? Where would I get the money to repair this vehicle? True, I didn't understand the problem, but I could tell even with my limited knowledge that the problem was big. Indeed, as I later learned, it was going to cost me a

22. The **Wilderness** Experience.

fortune to find a cylinder head and other related parts to put the engine back in running condition.

I slept without incident that night. In the morning I woke up thinking help would come early but that was simply wishful thinking. It was not until late in the afternoon that Mr Moyo, my good friend who works as a driver at the Zimbabwe Union Conference, driving a Fuso Canter truck owned by Pastor Maisva, came to tow me. Mr Moyo had helped me on many occasions. I thank God for people like him who will go out of their way to help, often at great expense to themselves. Arriving in Bulawayo late at night, we parked the 'sick' vehicle at the Zimbabwe Union Conference office and proceeded on to Solusi, arriving there after midnight. A week later I went back to town and arranged with a mechanic to fix the vehicle. Second-hand parts that were required could not be found in Zimbabwe. I sent word to Mr Orias Lungu, my Zambian mechanic, to look for the required parts. He quickly located them at his expense (I paid him later when I went to Zambia) and gave them to John, my kind-natured brother-in-law, who brought them.

After several weeks of work on the vehicle it was ready to be collected. We decided to test its strength and road worthiness on our trip to Zambia during my vacation in March 2006. Mwape, Mwila and John joined me on the trip. We travelled the more-than 1,000km to Lusaka without incident, until our arrival at my brother's home when one of the tubes on the radiator burst, causing all of the water to drain out of the engine. We thanked God that that had happened upon arrival, as it would have been a disaster had it occurred on the way. After a few days of rest in Lusaka, we took to the road again. That time our destination was Mansa, my ancestral home, to see Dad and other relatives. Because we started off late on Friday afternoon we drove up to Kapiri Mposhi, where we spent the Sabbath at my sister-in-law Christine's place. Christine and her husband Fred had recently moved from Lusaka to Kapiri Mposhi where Fred was running a petrol station.

At Kapiri Mposhi it was my pleasure to visit my long-time friend and colleague Pastor Patrick N'gandwe whom I have nicknamed 'Chikolokoto'. His wife Diana was happy to see me. We reminisced about our days together at Rusangu Ministerial School where I served as a teacher while Patrick was a student. His wife often invited me for meals, since I was a bachelor for most of the time I was there. Pastor and Mrs N'gandwe had

The Day My World Caved In.

since become senior members of the Copperbelt Field ministerial force.

On Sabbath I drove with Pastor N'gandwe to the Kapiri Central church where he had asked me to preach. At the small church I stumbled into Elder and Mrs Sianagowa, dear elderly friends I had made in Chingola where I married Martha. Stumbling into those wonderful people was an emotional moment. When Mrs Sianagowa saw me she couldn't hold back her tears. We held each other as she sobbed in silence. I understood why. The Sianagowas acted as my parents in Chingola. It was actually at their home that Martha and I spent the first night of our honeymoon. It was at their home that all the wedding preparations on my side were made. Their daughter Mutinta was one of the flower girls at our wedding. Mutinta is now a big girl with a home of her own. Mr Sianagowa had been a deputy headmaster at Chingola High School for a number of years before he left for Botswana where he secured a teaching post. Since we parted company – more than ten years earlier – we had not had an opportunity to bump into one another. That was the first time we had made contact since they had heard of Martha's death. It was therefore natural that the good lady, Mrs Sianagowa, would feel the way she did. It was indeed a low moment for all of us. Later that evening, I took my grown-up kids to be seen by their 'grandparents'.

Early Sunday morning, we started off for Mansa – Mwape, Mwila, John, and Mrs Diana N'gandwe who had joined us. Our journey was uneventful until our stopover along the Tuta Road at the scene of a nasty and fatal bus accident. The accident in which many passengers had lost their lives, according to eyewitnesses, had happened the previous day. The remains of the mangled bus looked as if it had been left there for half a century. It was hard to believe that anyone had survived. Later I learned that my friend, Baldwin Kabanda, who had been on that CR Carriers bus that was travelling from Mansa to Lusaka, had survived the accident. The front section was dangling in one direction while the back was in another. Passenger seats appeared as though they had been on fire, and their empty frames stood shattered and abandoned. I shuddered to imagine the agony of the last minutes of the ill-fated passengers. The bus had been moving at high speed when its right front tyre burst, causing the driver to lose control. The speeding vehicle – like a lion seeking whom to devour – went and hit a nearby tree.

We spent about ten minutes at the accident scene before we started

22. The **Wilderness** Experience.

off. After about two kilometres I noticed the temperature gauge on the meter suddenly rising. I immediately pulled the vehicle to the side and stopped. We opened the bonnet and discovered much to our dismay water from somewhere in the engine trickling down. Another rather tedious search revealed that a small rubber tube that carried water in the cooling system had burst. We had no mechanical ability to fix it so hoped for the arrival of a mechanic with a Good Samaritan heart. The scorching hot weather didn't help the situation. I calculated that tempers would soon be flying high, especially from the kids who had always complained about the idea of going to that boring place called Mansa where their Dad was born. The new generation could not see any sense in travelling such long distances almost every year just for their father to visit his boring humble dwelling. I tried to get everyone to relax and assured them that all would be OK under God, but my kids' faces showed they didn't care about that religious talk. They were tired and hungry. What they needed was physical relief and not a pep religious homily.

To break down on the Tuta Road is a terrible experience. There are very few motorists who use it, in spite of its being a good road. I will not go into the political reasons that necessitated its construction under the Kenneth Kaunda regime. After what seemed to the kids like a century of impatient waiting, a motorist at whom we waved stopped to find out what the problem was. One of the two men – the senior one – recognised me. He told us that he knew me as a pastor in the Adventist Church. He too was actually an Adventist. His driver with a knowledge of mechanics identified the problem and fixed it. After putting water in the radiator, we thanked the kind man, gave him a token of appreciation and started off. I saw my kids' faces brightening up. However, as the speed began to increase I saw the temperature gauge rising. We had to stop. Pressure had built up in the radiator and thick vapour was coming through one of the points in the engine. We rested for a while and put more water in the radiator and started off. As soon as the speed began to exceed 40kph, the temperature began to rise again. From where we had that breakdown to Mansa, our destination, was almost 300km. At the normal speed of 100kph we should have arrived in Mansa by ten o'clock. By then, it was late in the afternoon and we were still very far from our destination. With the car crawling at that snail's pace of 20kph, only God knew what time we would reach Mansa if, indeed, we could make it. We kept stopping

The Day My World Caved In.

every ten or so kilometres to allow the engine to cool and to add more water. I have to thank God for John who had the strength of a youth to help with the disagreeable task of adding water in the radiator all the way.

At one point while I was driving I felt as though I was losing my breath. I was convinced that if that condition continued I was either going to faint or die. I asked John to help me drive the vehicle as I went and sat in the passenger seat behind. I was feeling helpless and knew that I was going to lose consciousness. I tried not to alarm the others by pretending that everything was OK, but I knew that it was just a matter of time before I collapsed. I told John that I was feeling weak without understanding the reason why. John told me he was having the same feeling. We stopped to look for water. I opened the door and staggered out. Fortunately, there was a village just close by. Though it was night-time, people hadn't yet gone to bed. We walked to a nearby house and asked for water. Even though it was dark I could see dark marks on the container holding water. It was just lying outside. Our kind host picked a cup from the floor – only heaven knew how dirty it was – and poured water in it from the dirty container and gave it me to drink. I was thirsty; hygiene was the last thing on my mind. There is a saying in my language that the rules of hygiene affect only those who know about them. I emptied the contents of that dirty cup into my mouth as every organ in my body that had been longing for water gave a sigh of relief. Minutes later I started feeling better. It was then that I discovered what the problem was. I had not drunk any water in the intense heat we had endured the whole day.

We arrived in Mansa around midnight. The following morning John took the vehicle to a local mechanic who flushed the radiator with some chemical, removing a lot of dirt in the process. The procedure did help to cool the temperature, though it did not solve the problem completely. A week later on our way back to Lusaka we experienced heating problems all the way, though our speed had improved from that of a snail to a donkey. Back in Lusaka I took the vehicle to my mechanic who diagnosed two problems. Both the radiator and the cylinder head needed to be replaced. Because of the huge expense needed in replacing the cylinder head, the mechanic suggested an alternative – paying in instalments. And that's what we ended up doing. I had to pay through the nose to have

22. The **Wilderness** Experience.

those two things done. The money I should have used for things I had budgeted for was used to repair that vehicle which from the outside looked really good. I felt stressed and wondered why God kept allowing problem after problem to come my way in such quick succession.

A few days later I flew from Lusaka to Blantyre, Malawi, for a camp meeting. The Kabula Hill Adventist church in Blantyre had invited me to be their guest speaker during their annual camp meeting. The problems I had been going through left me with hardly any strength to prepare for the meetings. Earlier on, I had told God that what I needed was a holiday and not another stressful week of meetings. At Chileka International Airport in Blantyre, I found my friend Enwell Kadango waiting for me. We drove to his mansion where his wife and children received me with what I can only describe as a hero's welcome. As it was already suppertime, we found the table set with a variety of nicely prepared dishes a starving man like me would appreciate. I laughed to myself to think of the diet I had been used to back home in Zimbabwe and the food that lay before me. What a contrast! After the sumptuous evening meal, we chatted a bit before I retired to my room which had been elegantly prepared. That night as I went to sleep, I was just so happy to forget about the endless financial problems I had been going through.

That week in Blantyre afforded me with the rest I sorely needed. I was showered with love, good company, so much appreciation and satisfying meals. While the people of Kabula thought they had invited me for meetings, I knew that God had other things in mind. God wanted me to take a rest from all the problems I had been going through. God knew that the best place in the whole world for me to take that break was at Kabula Hill in Blantyre, Malawi.

I wish that I could mention the names of all the people God used to make that happen, but I might forget a name or two. I can only say 'thank you' to my family of Kabula Hill Adventist church for hosting me.

I flew back to Lusaka and a few days later I was on my way to Solusi. The vehicle, thankfully, performed very well all the 1000km I had to cover from Lusaka to Solusi.

One Sabbath while preaching at Highlands church in Harare, I mentioned that it had cost me about eight Zimbabwean dollars as bride price for my beautiful wife Martha. Everyone laughed. It didn't make sense that such a beautiful girl could be 'priced' so low. Well, the thing is

The Day My World Caved In.

that at the time I told the story, the Zimbabwean dollar was very strong compared to the Zambian kwacha which had tumbled quite low. But now there was a reversal of fortunes. The economy in Zambia was growing. Inflation had come down to a single digit while that of Zimbabwe was soaring at more than 14, 000% (figure quoted from *The Standard*, of 2-8 December 2007, a weekly private newspaper in Zimbabwe), the highest in the world. There is a lesson here for all the nations of the world. Things fall apart. I know for a fact that there was a time when Zambia had a very strong economy – in fact so strong that in the southern region only South Africa was ahead. That was the time of the booming copper industry. Zambia was indeed an economic powerhouse. The country was able to provide its citizenry with free education from primary to university level. And we had free medical services. That was the time when a lot of money also went into helping all our other neighbours who hadn't yet attained independence: Angola, Mozambique, Namibia, South Africa and Zimbabwe. And then the country got broke! But Zambia never reached the level of poverty in Zimbabwe. I can say this for a fact, because I have lived in both countries during some of their worst economic crises.

As the Zimbabwean scenario kept passing through my mind, I saw a guy selling boiled eggs. I was hungry and needed something to eat. I stopped him and asked how much he was selling the eggs at. 'Z$50, 000,' he said. I couldn't believe my ears. How in the world can you sell a boiled egg at fifty thousand dollars? As I write this, that figure has more than tripled. Because I was hungry, I ended up buying two eggs for one hundred thousand dollars!

A word about my friends the Chimukas is in order here. David, a fellow of the Royal College of Surgeons (South Africa), is a cardiovascular thoracic surgeon at Parirenyatwa Hospital in Harare and also runs his own practice. David, unlike most doctors I know, is loud and very outgoing. It's difficult to tell that he is a doctor who has even reached the distinction of dropping the title 'doctor' from his name. He is unassuming, natural, down-to-earth and mingles with all people very freely. He is a very generous man. One time when I was to conduct meetings in Bulawayo, he took me to the airport and my luggage was overweight. I didn't have cash to pay that extra charge. David just asked how much they were asking, and, even though it was quite a huge sum, he paid without even thinking about it. His wife Vangrista is also outgoing

22. The **Wilderness** Experience.

and generous. One time a group of us from Zambia (Pardon and Judith Mwansa, Goodwell and Rhoda Nthani, and my wife Martha and I) decided to buy a gift to present to the Chimukas to show our appreciation for their generosity. Unfortunately, we somehow got distracted and never got to fulfil that intention. The Chimukas had been so good, kind and generous to all of us that we felt just saying 'thank you' wasn't enough. By the way, David was one of the people who drove from Harare to attend the funeral of my wife Martha.

I arrived in Bulawayo that morning and rested briefly at a friend's house before proceeding to Solusi. Our seminar commenced the following day. Arrangements were made to pick me up from my house in the afternoon to drive to the meetings at the Large City Hall in Bulawayo. After the meetings, I went for supper to Mr and Mrs Mazinyane's home, after which I was driven back to Solusi. The two weeks were indeed hectic. I had lectures in the morning and afternoon and a seminar in the evening. The two-week-long seminar was well attended. There was also plenty of good music.

Music became my part-time preoccupation for a good part of the year 2007. Late in the evening I would rehearse, using the various sound tracks I had recorded over the years. I had decided to do some recording some day and needed to be ready adequately for that task. I also decided, as a way to pick myself up, to do a few concerts around and about. It was a funny scene each evening as I fully exercised my lungs, trying to bring my voice to a suitable standard. At times I felt so tired and with no motivation to sing that I just wanted to sleep. However, I would, even under those extreme circumstances, muster sufficient strength to rehearse. Beginning such sessions was indeed a challenge. Often I would tell myself that I would practise only one or two songs, but after singing one song I would encourage myself to go on with another one and another one. Before long I was back on track and went on to finish the whole session, usually lasting for more than two hours. My voice improved and I began to gain some measure of confidence. I therefore decided to put that practice to the test by organising a concert at the City Centre Adventist church in Bulawayo. On the day of the concert I prayed that God would help me to honour his name by my performing in a manner that would draw many to Christ. I asked him to stand by my side, especially in view of the fact that I had not done any singing since my

The Day My World Caved In.

wife died two years previously. If the concert were to be judged by the number of the people who attended, it would be described as fairly successful. Later in the same year, I organised a concert at the University of Zambia Medical School in Lusaka and another at Mazabuka's Central Adventist church. Plans were also under way to do a concert at Solusi University.

I also tried my hand at the music-making software 'Fruity Loops'. I found it quite fascinating that one could make music digitally on the computer. I created several sound tracks that even shocked me. It was a nice feeling to know that with some effort I could actually create my own sound tracks. In the past they have been done by my gifted friend Gideon Kasozi, who owns a studio in Kampala, Uganda. In the new job of teaching where travelling wasn't a factor, it wasn't possible to continue working with Gideon. It was, therefore, a welcome relief for me to know that I could actually create my own sound tracks if I threw some of my time into the venture.

Of all the things I did at Solusi, teaching was the most exciting and rewarding venture. I counted it a privilege that God would give me such a lofty assignment. I always prayed for guidance, strength, wisdom and insight. While I looked lost, disoriented and lonely along Solusi's paths, inside the classroom I found my real self. I thoroughly enjoyed every moment. Indeed, I was being paid to do what I enjoyed doing most. And while it can be said that Solusi was a wilderness where the heat of affliction was my constant companion, it was also a place where God began to mend my broken heart.

I must also mention that every single time I was on holiday I travelled to Zambia. Sometimes I was alone and at other times I was with my children. I should like to thank my sister-in-law, Mrs Catherine Kasongo, and her husband, for being there for me and my children. Many times when we visited Lusaka it was at their place that we stayed. They looked after us very well. My good friends May and Mwewa Chibende also gave me shelter at those times when I chose to stay with them. I thank them for being generous and so accommodating, often at very short notice. A friend in need is a friend indeed. At other times my friend Chriticles Mwansa, Zambia Revenue Authority Commissioner General, also provided open doors to his home. Several times I stayed at his place. When I extended my visits to Kitwe, my dear friends Alice and Bodwin Chishimba

22. The **Wilderness** Experience.

provided shelter and food. They always looked forward to my visits and never tired of looking after me. I wish these friends and others whom I have not mentioned God's rich blessings. May their tribes increase.

At the time of writing, it is towards the end of December 2007. Life has moved on. If God grants me life, I intend to marry early in 2008. But before I can bring this story to a close, I need to get back to the loving life that was tragically taken away on 6 March in 2005. It is because of the sudden end of that life that this book was conceived and written. I shall briefly turn to that life in the next chapter which also, incidentally, brings the story of *The Day My World Caved In* to an end.

The Day My World Caved In.

chapter 23

Who Was Martha Mwansa?

Who was Martha Mwansa? Martha was born to Jacob and Ruth Saini of Mwense, Zambia, on 5 May 1965. She attended Mansa Secondary School, after which she trained as a nurse at Nchanga School of Nursing. She also trained as a secretary. After we came to Harare she worked as a secretary in the Personal Ministries and Stewardship departments of the Eastern Africa Division of Seventh-day Adventists. While working, she also studied and completed by long distance a Bachelor of Business Administration degree with Thames Valley University in England in 2002. At the time of her death in March 2005, she had been working as an accountant in the insurance office of the Treasury department of the Southern Africa-Indian Ocean Division.

However, the question of who she was cannot be answered in the statements above. Martha was a wonderful loving wife. I was always proud of her and never ceased wondering how God could bring such a loving person into my life. While she became the ideal helpmate, she did not lose her individuality. She was a woman truly made in the image of God. She created such a loving and lovely atmosphere at home that it was always a joy to be there. If I forgot to notify her that I had visitors I was bringing home, she wasn't one to castigate me after they had gone. I could count on her counsel for something I was not clear about regarding the will of God. If she had a challenging situation she wanted to discuss with me, she would begin by praying over it before she would bring it to my attention. She bore patiently with my childish habits of leaving things

23. Who Was Martha Mwansa?

in the wrong places: socks, shoes, shirts, jackets and other things one dare not mention. She was simply an amazing woman.

I never knew her to be voluble on moral issues, yet she lived a morally pure life. She did not make a show of reading the Bible, yet she read it regularly. She had a large heart that loved people. There were times I was in those moods when I did not appreciate being disturbed by unwanted visitors. Martha was always there to welcome such people. Our house was almost always full. Whenever Dad was visiting she would take time to chat with him while I went to hide myself on the pretext that I was busy doing something.

We were unfortunate not to have had the opportunity of having Mum come to visit us while we lived in Harare, because her illness couldn't allow her to do so. One day we received word that Mum had suffered a stroke. We travelled to Mansa, Zambia, where she and Dad lived. I will forever be grateful for the care Martha gave Mum. Mum could not speak and she had problems using one of her legs and hands. Often she would lie outside under a mango tree. Martha would just be there with her, helping to fix her pillow or turn her from one side to the other. She would also help her walk to the nearby clinic to get her injections. She would prepare her food and just help her with nearly everything she needed. One day while I was contemplating her kindness to my ailing mum, tears started to roll down my cheeks. I could not understand what type of a woman Martha was. After coming back from that trip, I wrote Martha a letter in which I expressed my appreciation for the way she had taken care of her mother-in-law.

Honestly, I did not deserve to be honoured in that way by God. Whenever we travelled home, Martha would get different kinds of gifts for my mum, aunties and other family members.

Martha had a way with kids that always humbled me. Her patience with them never ceased to amaze me. I prayed often that I could have a heart like that. Martha was the one person I had met who convinced me beyond doubt that it is possible in this life to experience what our Lord Jesus describes as being born again. She was simply the best example I had come across that demonstrated what I could not find even in my own life. While I don't remember hearing her preach a sermon about being born again, she nevertheless revealed it. Through her life, God showed me that it is possible in this life to be converted.

The Day My World Caved In.

Martha loved to volunteer wherever and whenever she found an opportunity. It was so natural to her to offer herself in situations that needed help. She was a true servant of the people.

At church I cannot remember a year when she just went to church to do nothing but worship God. She always had many assignments. On Sabbath she was involved with children's programmes and on Sunday she helped at children's services. I often wondered where she got the strength to do all those things. At the end of Sabbath services she was never the one to go straight to the car. She always took time to find out how people were doing. I usually greeted a few people and went to the car to wait. Many times I found it boring to go back for the Sabbath afternoon programmes but Martha always faithfully attended.

Martha kept in touch with many church members. She always attended a funeral. If she was aware that someone was sick, she often visited. Just before she took the trip that finally claimed her life in Zambia, she had written a note to a Zambian woman living in Harare, discussing a visit to the hospital to see the then Zambian High Commissioner to Zimbabwe, Professor Mumba (who also died a few weeks after Martha's death). I was the type who often just got dragged into situations, and she was the exact opposite.

In our home Marha was responsible for our finances. She performed her duties so well that I virtually left that side of our affairs to her. She banked the money, withdrew what needed to be withdrawn and paid those who needed to be paid.

Martha was a disciplined spirit when it came to whatever her hand found to do. When she enrolled for a degree course in business administration, she was a full-time mother, looking after two primary school kids, a full-time employee of the Adventist Church and a full-time homemaker. How she found time to play each of those roles without breaking down is something only God can explain. Within four years of study, she successfully completed her degree in business administration from Thames Valley University. The then director of education at the Southern Africa-Indian Ocean Division, Dr Tommy Nkungula, was so impressed with her achievement of being a mother, wife and employee that he suggested that she be put on scholarship to study for an MBA at Solusi University. She declined at that time because she wanted a bit of a break from academic pressure.

23. Who Was Martha Mwansa?

Was she perfect? No. But I can say, having lived with her, that I never saw any negative thing in her life that stood as something I confronted time and again. I speak honestly here. I cannot remember a single negative trait that had taken root in her life. It's hard actually to remember seeing her lose her temper and say things that were unpalatable. It is much easier to see faults in a person whom you live with than it is to see good things. I must confess that the opposite was true in Martha's life. This, then, was the angel God gave me the opportunity to live with for sixteen years.

Ever since she left us my prayer has been that God would give me a double portion of her spirit. I have wept many times before the presence of God to have Martha's wonderful life reproduced in me. With my own eyes, for sixteen years, I witnessed the power of God in her transformed life. Many times the people who appear to be born again are only those whom we read about in the Bible. For me, I did witness a transformed life outside the Bible. May the Lord, I pray, give me a double portion of that woman's spirit.

About six years before she died she had a remarkable dream that she shared with me. One night she found herself sitting with God. As the two were relaxing together, God took an album and began to show her pictures of some of the faithful ones who had died in the faith. Martha said that she saw many people there. God would take a picture and then he would show it to her. They were beautiful pictures, she said. Then something that stunned her happened. God took out Martha's picture and showed it to her. She said that she felt the kind of excitement that cannot be explained but only experienced. 'Honey, I was excited and so happy to see my picture in God's photo album of his faithful ones who have gone to sleep,' she told me as she narrated the story the following morning. Today I think about that dream and ponder its significance. Could it be that God was reassuring her that even though her life would be cut short some day, her place in Paradise had been secured? I don't know, but I certainly shall look for her when the saints will be marching in God's glorious Paradise.

'Then I saw a new heaven and a new earth, for the first heaven and the first earth had passed away, and there was no longer any sea. I saw the Holy City, the New Jerusalem, coming down out of heaven from God, prepared as a bride beautifully dressed for her husband. And I heard a

The Day My World Caved In.

loud voice from the throne saying, "Now the dwelling of God is with men, and he will live with them. They will be his people, and God Himself will be with them and be their God. He will wipe every tear from their eyes. There will be no more death or mourning or crying or pain, for the old order of things has passed away." ' (Revelation 21:1-4.)

Then will the dark day turn into the eternal day of joy.

May that day come soon.